# Contents

## Introduction 3
What this book contains 3
What the National Tests in mathematics cover 3
What levels do these practice papers cover? 3
Helping your child sit tests 4
Setting the mental tests 4
Setting the written papers 5
What to do with the results 5

## Formulae 6

## Mental tests 7
Mental Test 1 7
Student answer sheets for Mental Test 1 9
Mental Test 2 11
Student answer sheets for Mental Test 2 13

## Written papers 15
Practice questions at Level 3 15
Paper 1 (Levels 4–6) 21
Paper 2 (Levels 5–7) 36
Practice questions at Level 8 50

## Answers 54
Mental Test 1 54
Mental Test 2 55
Practice questions at Level 3 56
Paper 1 57
Paper 2 59
Practice questions at Level 8 61
National Curriculum levels 62

Text © ST(P), Gill Hewlett, 1999

The right of ST(P) and Gill Hewlett to be identified as authors of this work has been asserted by them in accordance with the Copyright, Designs and Patents Act 1988.

All rights reserved. No part of this publication may be reproduced or transmitted in any form or by any means, electronic or mechanical, including photocopy, recording or any information storage and retrieval system, without permission in writing from the publisher or under licence from the Copyright Licensing Agency Limited. Further details of such licences (for reprographic reproduction) may be obtained from the Copyright Licensing Agency Limited of 90 Tottenham Court Road, London W1P 9HE.

This edition published exclusively for WHSmith, 1999, by
Stanley Thornes (Publishers) Ltd
Ellenborough House
Wellington Street
CHELTENHAM
GL50 1YW

99 00 01 02 \ 10 9 8 7 6 5 4 3 2 1

A catalogue record for this book is available from the British Library

ISBN 0-7487-5225-0

Designed by Rocket Design Ltd, London

Illustrated by Peters & Zabransky, Sevenoaks, Kent

Typeset by Pentacor PLC, High Wycombe, Bucks

Printed and bound in Spain by Mateu Cromo

# Introduction

## What this book contains

During your child's third year in secondary school (Year 9) he or she will sit Key Stage 3 National Assessment Tests in the three core subjects: English, mathematics and science. These tests take place in school over a period of about a week during May and results are reported back to you. For each of the three subjects your child will be given a mark in the form of a level. Most children will perform in the range of Levels 4–6 by the end of Key Stage 3, with an average performance being roughly Level 5.

The tests are a valuable measure of your child's performance over the first three years of secondary school and give an indication of their likely performance at Key Stage 4, which leads to the GCSE examinations.

This book provides practice papers and questions in mathematics to be used to help prepare your child to sit the tests in this subject confidently. The papers will:

- provide test questions similar to those in the National Tests for Key Stage 3 of the National Curriculum;
- give your child practice in sitting the tests: working to a set time, getting familiar with the format and style of the tests and developing effective test strategies;
- give a broad guide to your child's likely level of performance;
- give you an idea of strengths and weaknesses in your child's learning.

## What the National Tests in mathematics cover

The National Curriculum for mathematics at Key Stage 3 is divided into four areas called 'attainment targets'.

The four attainment targets are:

1 Using and Applying Mathematics
2 Number and Algebra
3 Shape, Space and Measures
4 Handling Data

The first attainment target, Using and Applying Mathematics, involves practical work and investigations relating to the other three attainment targets. It does not form part of the National Tests but is assessed by the school.

For the tests in May your child will probably sit three papers. Two of these will be ordinary written papers (one of which will be a 'no calculator' paper) and the third will be a mental test. There are four tiers of entry: National Curriculum Levels 3–5, 4–6, 5–7 and 6–8.

## What levels do these practice papers cover?

For ease of use and also to give a student as much practice as possible, this book contains two written tests and two mental tests. These cover the most popular tiers of entry at Levels 4–6 and 5–7. Separate practice questions at Level 3 and Level 8 are also provided. Paper 1 contains 15 questions, five questions at each of the levels covered. Questions 1–5 are at Level 4, 6–10 at Level 5 and 11–15 at Level 6. Paper 2 has 14 questions. Questions 1–5 are at Level 5, 6–9 at Level 6 and 10–14 at Level 7. There are five practice questions at Level 3 and six at Level 8. Questions where a calculator is allowed are marked by a symbol.

Mental Test 1 is aimed at the expected level of attainment for students at Level 4.

Mental Test 2 is aimed at the expected level of attainment for students at Levels 5–6.

# Introduction

## Helping your child sit tests

As well as practising mathematics, one of the key aims of this book is to give your child practice in working under test conditions. All the tests are timed and your child should try to complete each one within the given time. In order to make the best use of the tests, and to ensure that the experience is a positive one for your child, it is helpful to follow a few basic principles:

1 Talk with your child first before beginning the tests. Present the activity positively and reassuringly. Encourage your child to consider the papers as an activity which will help, always making him or her feel secure about the process. Remember that an average student will not have studied all the topics included in these tests.

2 Ensure that your child is relaxed and rested before doing a test. It may be better to do a paper at the weekend or during the holidays rather than straight after a day at school.

3 Find a quiet place, free from noise or disturbance, for doing the tests.

4 Ensure that there is a watch or clock available (with a second hand when doing the mental tests). Your child will also need:

- a pencil and a ruler;
- a calculator, preferably a scientific calculator, but there should be a $\sqrt{}$ key;
- a protractor or angle measurer.
- compasses

5 Progress through the tests in the order of the levels. Be positive about what your child achieves. Remember that an average student at Key Stage 3 is only at Level 5 but these papers include material up to Level 8.

6 Ensure that your child understands exactly what to do for each paper and give some basic strategies for tackling the task. For example:

- Try to tackle all the questions but don't worry if you can't do some. Put a pencil mark by any you can't do, leave them and come back to them at the end.
- Make sure you read the questions carefully.
- Refer to the formula sheet on page 6.
- If you have any time over at the end, go back and check your answers.

7 Taking time to talk over a test beforehand and to discuss any difficulties afterwards will help your child to become more confident at sitting tests.

8 Whatever your child achieves, ensure that you give plenty of praise for effort.

## Setting the mental tests

You can use the mental tests before or after the written papers. Your child will probably find them quite challenging if they have not attempted anything similar before. For this reason there are two answer sheets for each test. It is suggested that you start with Mental Test 1 to be answered on sheet 1A. A few days later try the same test again, giving your child sheet 1B for recording the answers. If your child coped fairly well with Mental Test 1, try Mental Test 2 in the same way. You will need to remove the answer sheets from the book to give to your child.

Before you begin, it would be helpful to practise the following skills with your child:

- tables up to $10 \times 10$;
- adding and subtracting mentally, for example: $18 + 7$ or $36 - 12$;
- strategies such as 'to get $80 - 48$, first do $80 - 50$, then add 2';
- for Level 5, multiply or divide a number, including a decimal, by 10, 100 or 1000; for example: $34 \div 10$ or $7.5 \times 100$;
- for Level 7, check calculations by rounding to one significant figure; for example: $3145 \div 5.7$ is about 3000 divided by 6, which is 500.

You will need to ensure that you read the questions to your child within the set time.

## Introduction

### Setting the written papers

Try starting with the Level 3 practice questions, which should take about 15 minutes. Allow your child 20 minutes maximum. If your child finds these relatively easy, then give him or her Paper 1. Allow the student one hour to complete this. If your child completes Paper 1 then let him or her try all or part of Paper 2. Allow one hour for Paper 2 as well. Only attempt the Level 8 questions if your child gets close to Level 7 on Paper 2.

Before you begin, it would also be useful to make sure that when working on paper your child can:

- at Level 4, add and subtract decimals and do short multiplication and division by whole numbers; for example: set out properly and work out $3.6 + 15.2$ or $51 \times 7$;
- at Level 5, do long multiplication or long division by whole two-digit numbers; for example: set out properly and work out $68 \times 27$ or $598 \div 23$.

### What to do with the results

The tests in this book and the results gained from them are only a guide to your child's likely level of performance. They are not an absolute guarantee of how your child will perform in the National Tests themselves. However, these papers will at least allow your child to gain practice in sitting tests; they will also give you an insight into the strengths and weaknesses in their learning.

If there are particular areas of performance which seem weaker, it may be worth providing more practice of the skills required. It is also valuable to discuss any such weaknesses with your child's subject teacher, and to seek confirmation of any problem areas and advice on how to proceed. It is always better to work in partnership with the school if you can. Above all ensure that you discuss these issues with your child in a positive and supportive way so that you have their co-operation in working together to improve learning.

# Formulae

You may need to use some of these formulae.

## Area

**Circle**

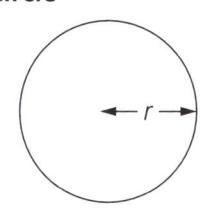

$\pi r^2$

Take $\pi$ as 3.14 or use the $\pi$ key on your calculator

**Rectangle**

length × width

**Triangle**

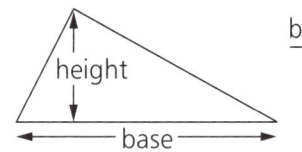

$\dfrac{base \times height}{2}$

**Parallelogram**

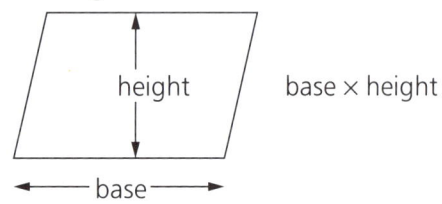

base × height

**Trapezium**

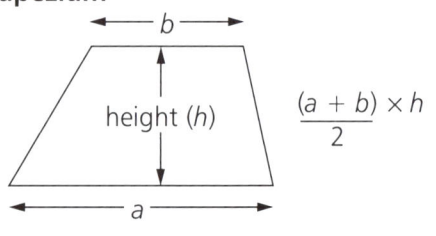

$\dfrac{(a + b) \times h}{2}$

## Length

**Circle**

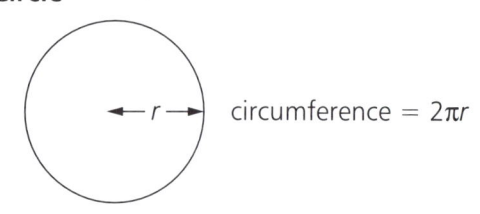

circumference = $2\pi r$

**For a right-angled triangle**

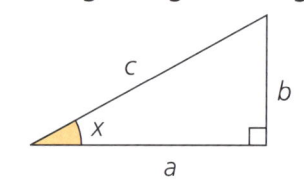

$a^2 + b^2 = c^2$ (Pythagoras' theorem)

$a = c \cos x$     $\cos x = \dfrac{a}{c}$

$b = c \sin x$     $\sin x = \dfrac{b}{c}$

$b = a \tan x$     $\tan x = \dfrac{b}{a}$

## Volume

**Prism**

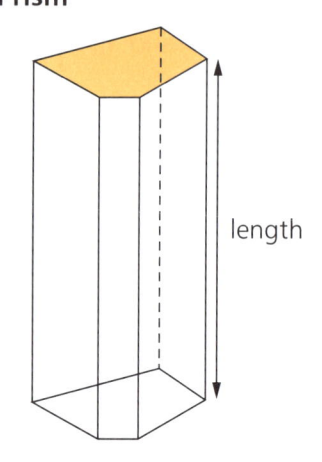

area of cross-section × length

# Mental Test 1

You will need a watch with a second hand.

The student should *only* have the answer sheet and a pen or pencil; calculators, rulers, erasers, and so on, are not allowed.

Read each question to the student twice.

The student then has the stated number of seconds to write the answer. Before you begin, explain to your child the following:

- you must work out the answers in your head – you can write numbers and calculations on your sheet but you are advised not to because of time restrictions;
- you must record each answer on the answer sheet, in the box alongside that question number;
- if you make a mistake, cross out the wrong answer and write the new answer alongside the box;
- it is quicker to write answers as numbers rather than words;
- if you cannot answer a question put a line in the box.

Now begin the test. (Remember to repeat each question.)

*You will have 5 seconds to answer each of these questions.*

1  What is half of sixty-eight?

2  How many metres are there in one kilometre?

3  Write the number which is halfway between thirty-two and thirty-three.

4  What is eight multiplied by six?

5  Write the number five thousand and fourteen in figures.

6  How many minutes in three hours?

7  What is four hundred and twenty subtract two hundred?

*You will have 10 seconds to answer each of these questions.*

8  Look at the spinner on your answer sheet. Is the spinner most likely to land on black, or white or grey?

9  What is the cost of three magazines at one pound fifteen pence each?

10  Look at the numbers on your answer sheet. Add them together.

11  What number is one hundred less than seven thousand?

## Mental test 1

**12** The pie chart on your answer sheet shows students' favourite subjects. Approximately what percentage prefer PE?

**13** Look at your answer sheet. What is the value of *p*?

**14** A coat costs sixty-two pounds. In a sale the coat costs twenty-seven pounds less. What is the sale price?

**15** A tape costs two pounds forty-nine pence. I buy two tapes. How much change do I get from ten pounds?

**16** How many minutes are three hundred and sixty seconds?

**17** The perimeter of a square is thirty-two centimetres. What is the length of each side?

**18** Subtract ten from two.

**19** Look at the rectangle on your answer sheet. What is its area?

**20** Look at the calculation on your answer sheet. Work out the answer.

**21** Look at the triangle on your answer sheet. What does the angle *a* measure?

**22** A pop concert ticket cost twenty-five pounds. The price went up by ten per cent. What is the new price?

**23** What is thirty-eight centimetres less than two metres? Give your answer in metres.

*You will have 15 seconds to answer each of these questions.*

**24** A film starts at eight-forty p.m. and lasts one hour forty-five minutes. What time does it end?

**25** Look at the shapes on your answer sheet. Which shape has rotational symmetry order four?

**26** Look at the numbers on your answer sheet. Circle the decimal that is nearest to three sevenths.

**27** Use the calculation on your answer sheet to help you work out the answer to ninety-six multiplied by four.

**28** What is the next prime number after thirty-one?

**29** Look at the circle on your answer sheet. Give an approximate value for the circumference.

**30** Look at the shape on your answer sheet. What is the area of a shape which is twice as wide and twice as long?

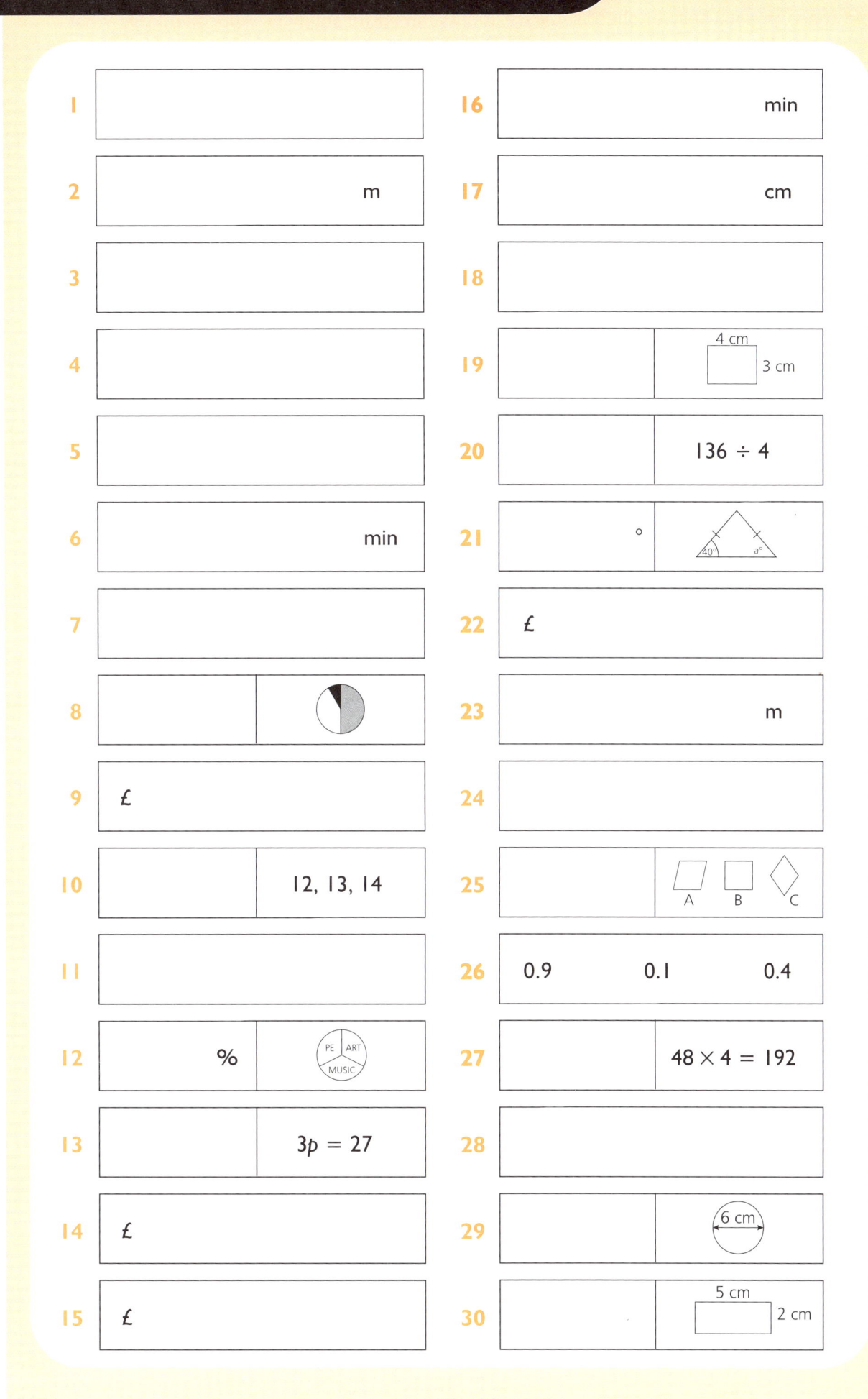

# Mental Test 1A
## Answer sheet

| | | | | |
|---|---|---|---|---|
| 1 | | 16 | | min |
| 2 | m | 17 | | cm |
| 3 | | 18 | | |
| 4 | | 19 | | 4 cm / 3 cm |
| 5 | | 20 | 136 ÷ 4 | |
| 6 | min | 21 | ° | 40°, a° |
| 7 | | 22 | £ | |
| 8 | (pie chart) | 23 | | m |
| 9 | £ | 24 | | |
| 10 | 12, 13, 14 | 25 | A B C | |
| 11 | | 26 | 0.9   0.1   0.4 | |
| 12 | % PE/ART/MUSIC | 27 | 48 × 4 = 192 | |
| 13 | 3p = 27 | 28 | | |
| 14 | £ | 29 | 6 cm | |
| 15 | £ | 30 | 5 cm / 2 cm | |

30

TOTAL (30)

9

# Mental Test 1B

## Answer sheet

| | | |
|---|---|---|
| 1 | | |
| 2 | m | |
| 3 | | |
| 4 | | |
| 5 | | |
| 6 | min | |
| 7 | | |
| 8 | |  |
| 9 | | |
| 10 | | 22, 23, 24 |
| 11 | | |
| 12 | % | ART<br>MUSIC<br>PE |
| 13 | | $5p = 60$ |
| 14 | £ | |
| 15 | £ | |

| | | |
|---|---|---|
| 16 | min | |
| 17 | cm | |
| 18 | | |
| 19 | | 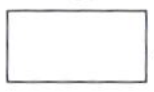4 cm<br>2 cm |
| 20 | | $152 \div 4$ |
| 21 | ° | 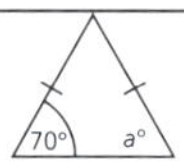70°<br>a° |
| 22 | £ | |
| 23 | m | |
| 24 | | |
| 25 | | 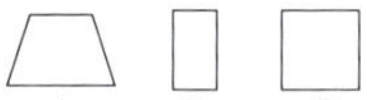A<br>B<br>C |
| 26 | 0.4 0.2 0.8 | |
| 27 | | $96 \times 2 = 192$ |
| 28 | | |
| 29 | | 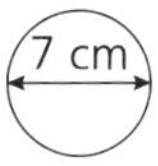7 cm |
| 30 | | 4 cm<br>2 cm |

30

TOTAL (30)

# Mental Test 2

You will need a watch with a second hand.

The student should *only* have the answer sheet and a pen or pencil; calculators, rulers, erasers, and so on, are not allowed.

Read each question to the student twice.

The student then has the stated number of seconds to write the answer. Before you begin, explain to your child the following:

- you must work out the answers in your head – you can write numbers and calculations on your sheet but you are advised not to because of time restrictions;
- you must record each answer on the answer sheet, in the box alongside that question number;
- if you make a mistake, cross out the wrong answer and write the new answer alongside the box;
- it is quicker to write answers as numbers rather than words;
- if you cannot answer a question put a line in the box.

Now begin the test. (Remember to repeat each question.)

*You will have 5 seconds to answer each of these questions.*

1. What is forty-eight multiplied by ten?

2. Write one fifth as a decimal.

3. There are four black cubes and six white cubes in a bag. I choose a cube at random. What is the probability that I choose a white cube?

4. How many centimetres are there in three and a half metres?

*You will have 10 seconds to answer each of these questions.*

5. What is three point eight added to four point six?

6. Twenty-five per cent of a number is fifteen. What is the number?

7. Look at the calculation on your answer sheet. Work out the answer.

8. Look at the expression on your answer sheet. Its value is thirty-two. Write an expression with a value of sixty-four.

9. Write a fraction that is equivalent to three quarters.

10. Look at the triangle on your answer sheet. What is the area of the triangle?

11. Look at the equation on your answer sheet. If $p$ is five, what is $q$?

## Mental test 2

**12** For one paper round, the probability that the newspaper is delivered before eight o'clock is nought point eight five. What is the probability that the newspaper is delivered after eight o'clock?

**13** The mean of *x*, *y* and *z* is ten. If *x* is eight and *y* is nine, what is *z*?

**14** Look at the equation on your answer sheet. Write down one possible value of *y*.

**15** Look at the expression on your answer sheet. Multiply out this expression.

**16** Write an approximate answer to the calculation on your answer sheet.

**17** If a safety light flashes thirty times in a minute how many times will it flash in one hour?

**18** Look at your answer sheet. What is the value of *n* if it is a whole number?

*You will have 15 seconds to answer each of these questions.*

**19** Arrange the numbers four, eight and five to make the largest possible even number.

**20** Look at the ages on your answer sheet. Put a circle around the median age.

**21** Use the calculation on your answer sheet to help you work out the answer to twenty-eight multiplied by eight point two.

**22** What is seventeen multiplied by eight?

**23** Two angles of a triangle are forty-three degrees and seventy-five degrees. How many degrees is the other angle?

**24** The sum of *x* and *y* is eleven. The product of *x* and *y* is twenty-eight. What are the values of *x* and *y*?

**25** Sixty-six metres per second is about the same as one hundred and fifty miles per hour. About how many miles per hour is forty-four metres per second?

**26** Look at the nets on your answer sheet. Circle the net which will fold up to make a cube.

**27** Look at the numbers on your answer sheet. Find the missing fraction.

**28** Multiply twenty-five by twenty-eight.

**29** Look at the shape on your answer sheet. What is the area of a shape whose area is two and a half times larger?

**30** Write down the value of one hundred and twenty divided by nought point two.

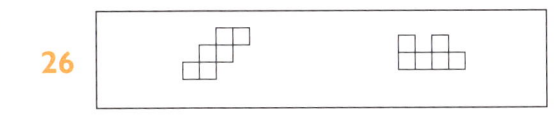

# Mental Test 2A
## Answer sheet

| | |
|---|---|
| 1 | |
| 2 | |
| 3 | |
| 4 | cm |
| 5 | |
| 6 | |
| 7 | $280 \div 7$ |
| 8 | $x + y$ |
| 9 | |
| 10 | 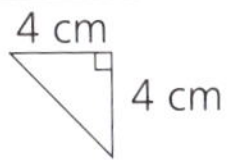 4 cm, 4 cm |
| 11 | $4p = q$ |
| 12 | |
| 13 | |
| 14 | $y^2 = 81$ |
| 15 | $x(4 - 2x)$ |
| 16 | $198 \times 42$ |
| 17 | |
| 18 | $14 < n < 16$ |
| 19 | |
| 20 | 17  21  13  18  22 |
| 21 | $28 \times 82 = 2296$ |
| 22 | |
| 23 | ° |
| 24 | |
| 25 | mph |
| 26 | |
| 27 | $\frac{1}{3} + \frac{1}{6} + ? = 1$ |
| 28 | |
| 29 | Area $= 12$ cm$^2$ |
| 30 | |

TOTAL (30)

# Mental Test 2B
## Answer sheet

| # | | | # | |
|---|---|---|---|---|
| 1 | | | 16 | $212 \times 38$ |
| 2 | | | 17 | |
| 3 | | | 18 | $26 < n < 28$ |
| 4 | cm | | 19 | |
| 5 | | | 20 | 12  17  18  10  15 |
| 6 | | | 21 | $28 \times 82 = 2296$ |
| 7 | $480 \div 6$ | | 22 | |
| 8 | $x - y$ | | 23 | ° |
| 9 | | | 24 | |
| 10 | 5 cm / 3 cm | | 25 | mph |
| 11 | $10p = 2q$ | | 26 | |
| 12 | | | 27 | $\frac{1}{2} + \frac{1}{6} + ? = 1$ |
| 13 | | | 28 | |
| 14 | $y^2 = 64$ | | 29 | Area = 15 cm² |
| 15 | $x(3 - 4x)$ | | 30 | |

TOTAL (30)

# Practice questions at Level 3

**20 Mins TIME ALLOWED**

The use of calculators is permitted if you see this symbol: ✓

This symbol: ✗ means you must not use a calculator.

## 1 Ice cream

9T were doing a survey about ice cream.

**ICE CREAMS**
Vanilla
Strawberry
Chocolate
Ripple
Toffee
Mint

Richard drew this pictogram to show people's favourite flavours.

| Flavour | Number of people |
|---|---|
| Vanilla | 🍦 |
| Strawberry | 🍦🍧 |
| Chocolate | 🍦🍦🍦🍦 |
| Ripple | 🍧 |
| Toffee | 🍦🍦🍦 |
| Mint | 🍦🍦 |

Key: 🍦 represents 2 people

a How many people prefer chocolate flavour ice cream?

_____

b How many people prefer strawberry flavour ice cream?

_____

c How many people were in the survey?

_____

TOTAL (3)

15

## Practice questions at Level 3

**d** 9A did the same survey in their class.

These are their results.

| Flavour | Number of people |
|---|---|
| Vanilla | 1 |
| Strawberry | 5 |
| Chocolate | 8 |
| Ripple | 4 |
| Toffee | 6 |
| Mint | 2 |

Draw a pictogram showing these results. Use 🍦 to represent 2 people.

## Practice questions at Level 3

**2 Times**

**a** Pauline is waiting for a bus.

Time now:

Next bus leaves at:

How long does Pauline have to wait for her bus? _____

**b** Charles is waiting for a train.

Time now: 07:15

Next train leaves at: 07:52

How long does Charles have to wait for his train? _____

**c** Angela is booking a journey on a ferry. She is taking her car.

|  |  | £ |
| --- | --- | --- |
| Mini-break | car + driver (5 days) | 45 |
| Saver | car + driver (10 days) | 61 |
| Flexible fare | car + driver (unlimited stay) | 81 |
| Adult | not driver | 9 |
| Child | (4–15 years) | 5 |

Find the cost of a 10-day trip for Angela and her 3 children aged 7, 9 and 14 years.

_____

TOTAL (3)

# Practice questions at Level 3

## 3 Number star

Start at 50.

Fill in the boxes:

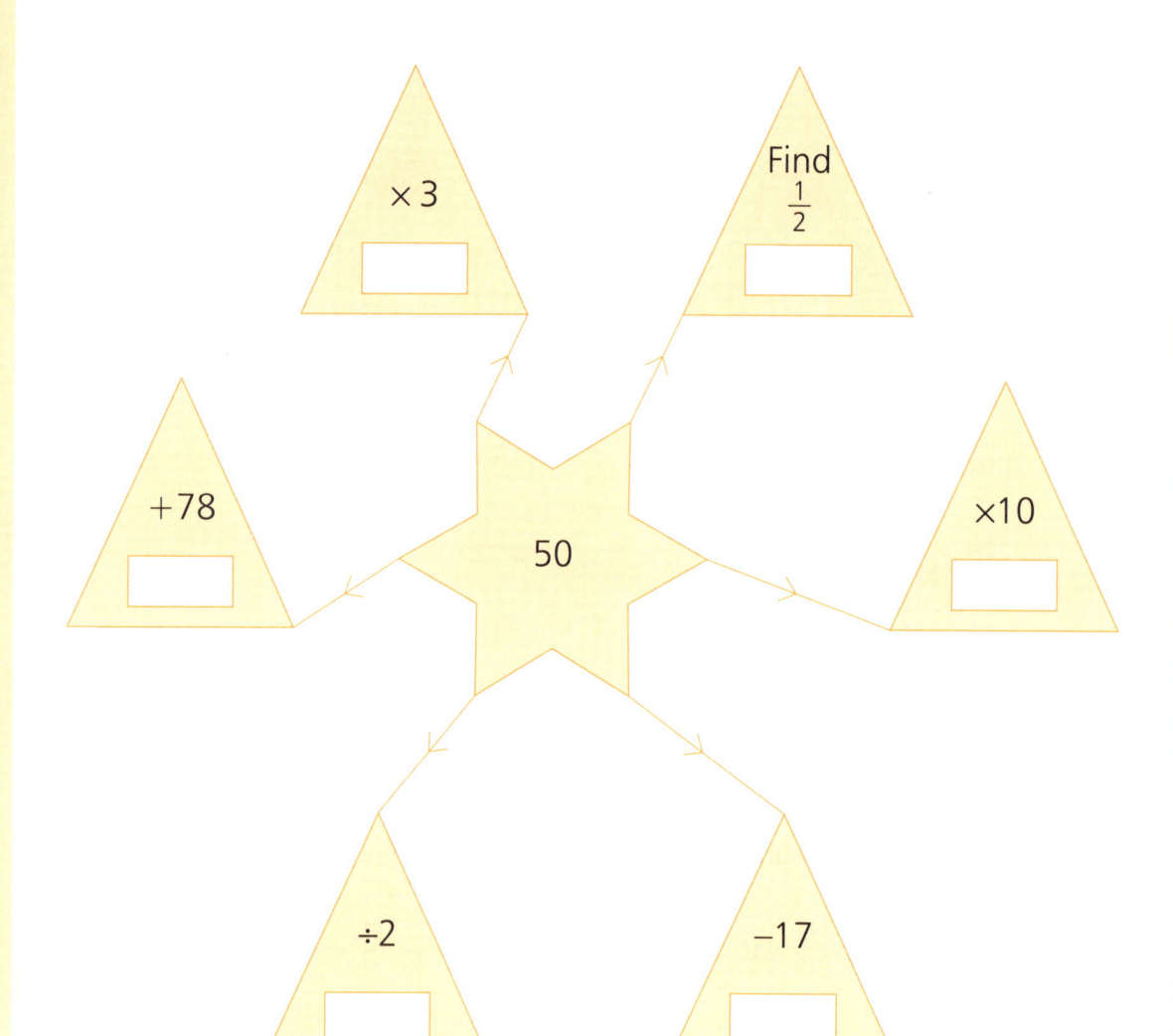

×3 ☐

Find $\frac{1}{2}$ ☐

+78 ☐

50

×10 ☐

÷2 ☐

−17 ☐

## Practice questions at Level 3

### 4 Game

Claire and Trevor are playing a number game. They take it in turns to turn up a card then move their counter by the number on the card. The first to get to either end wins.

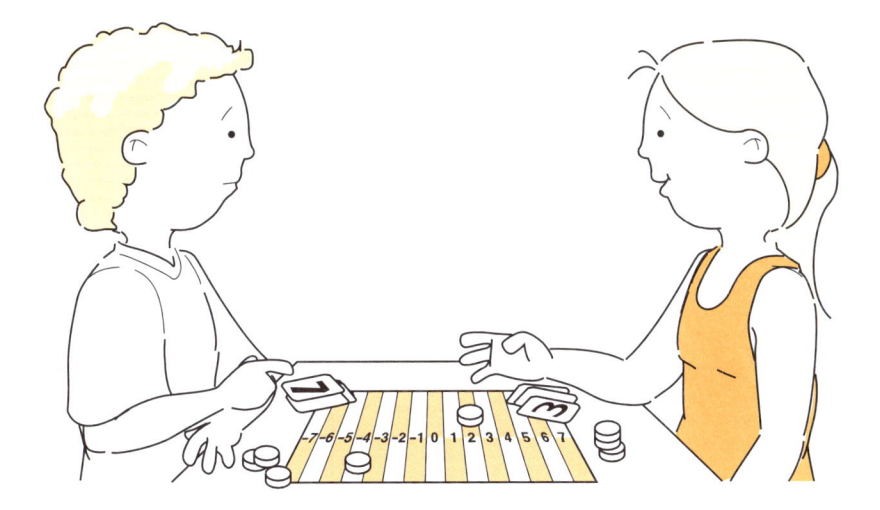

| −7 | −6 | −5 | −4 | −3 | −2 | −1 | 0 | 1 | 2 | 3 | 4 | 5 | 6 | 7 |
|---|---|---|---|---|---|---|---|---|---|---|---|---|---|---|
|  |  |  | T |  |  |  |  |  | C |  |  |  |  |  |

Trevor is on −4. He gets 8.

**a** Draw Trevor's counter on the table below after his go.

| −7 | −6 | −5 | −4 | −3 | −2 | −1 | 0 | 1 | 2 | 3 | 4 | 5 | 6 | 7 |
|---|---|---|---|---|---|---|---|---|---|---|---|---|---|---|
|  |  |  |  |  |  |  |  |  |  |  |  |  |  |  |

**b** Claire is on 2. On her next move she lands on −2. What card did she turn up?

_____

Draw where her counter lands on the same table.

**c** Which player is closer to an end? _____

TOTAL (3)

*Practice questions at Level 3*

### 5 Tiles

This tile shape has been tessellated to make a pattern.

**a** Complete the pattern below.

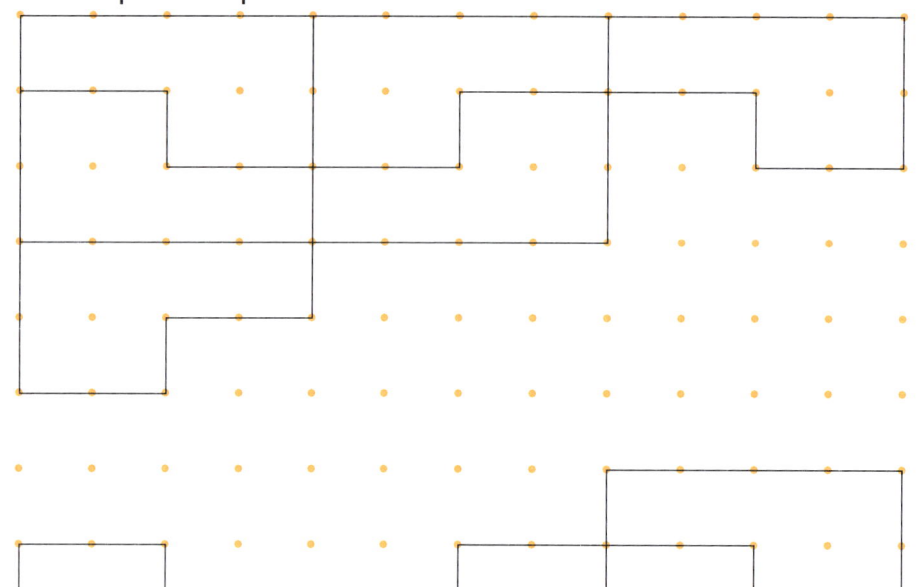

**b** How many tile shapes were used altogether in this pattern?

# Paper 1

## Test Paper 1    Levels 4–6

**60 Mins TIME ALLOWED**

The use of calculators is permitted in this paper if you see this symbol: ✓

This symbol: ✗ means you must not use a calculator.

### 1 Science

These results were collected by two pupils in a science experiment.

| Pupil A | |
|---|---|
| Time (s) | Water level (cm) |
| 0 | 16 |
| 1 | 14 |
| 2 | 12 |
| 3 | 9 |
| 4 | 6 |
| 5 | 3 |
| 6 | 1 |

| Pupil B | |
|---|---|
| Time (s) | Water level (cm) |
| 0 | 16 |
| 1 | 13 |
| 2 | 10 |
| 3 | 7 |
| 4 | 4 |
| 5 | 1 |
| 6 | 0 |

**a** Plot both sets of results as line graphs on these axes.

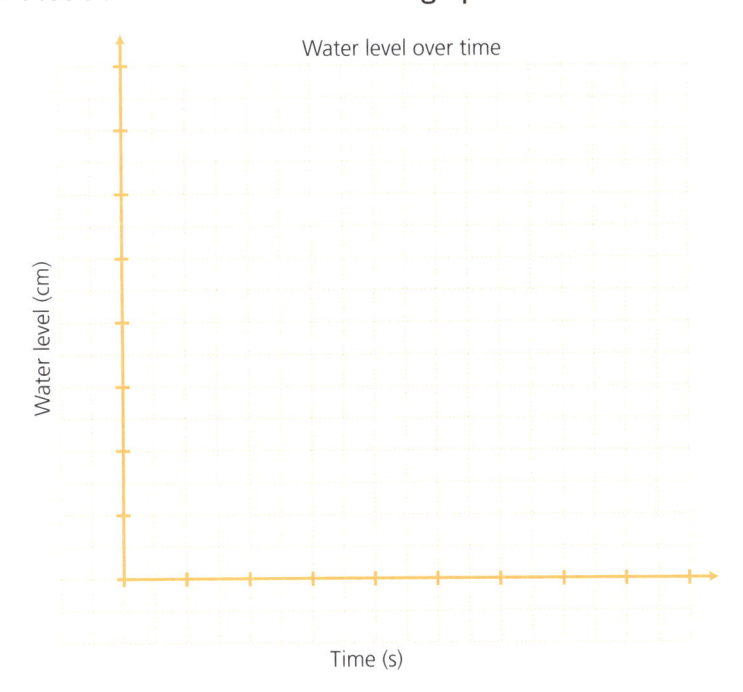

Water level over time

Water level (cm)

Time (s)

**b** How high was the water level to begin with? _____

**c** Write down one difference between the two sets of results.

_____

_____

TOTAL (5)

21

# Paper 1 test

**2 Bingo**

All these bingo cards have special numbers.

|   |   |   |   |   |
|---|---|---|---|---|
| 1 |   | 6 |   | 24 |
|   | 3 | 8 | 12 |   |
| 2 | 4 |   |   |   |

These numbers are factors of 24.

**a**

|   |   |   |   |   |
|---|---|---|---|---|
| 1 | 3 |   | 9 |   |
| 2 |   | 6 | 12 | 18 |
|   | 4 |   |   | 36 |

Write down what is special about these numbers:

_____

_____

**b**

|   |   |   |   |   |
|---|---|---|---|---|
| 5 |   | 20 |   | 45 |
|   | 10 |   | 30 |   |
|   |   | 25 |   |   |

Write down what is special about these numbers:

_____

_____

**c**

|   |   |   |   |   |
|---|---|---|---|---|
| 1 |   | 16 |   | 49 |
|   | 9 |   | 36 | 64 |
| 4 |   | 25 |   |   |

Write down what is special about these numbers:

_____

_____

TOTAL (3)

# Paper 1 test

## 3 Garden

This is a plan of Mr Smith's garden.

Scale: 1 cm : 5 metres

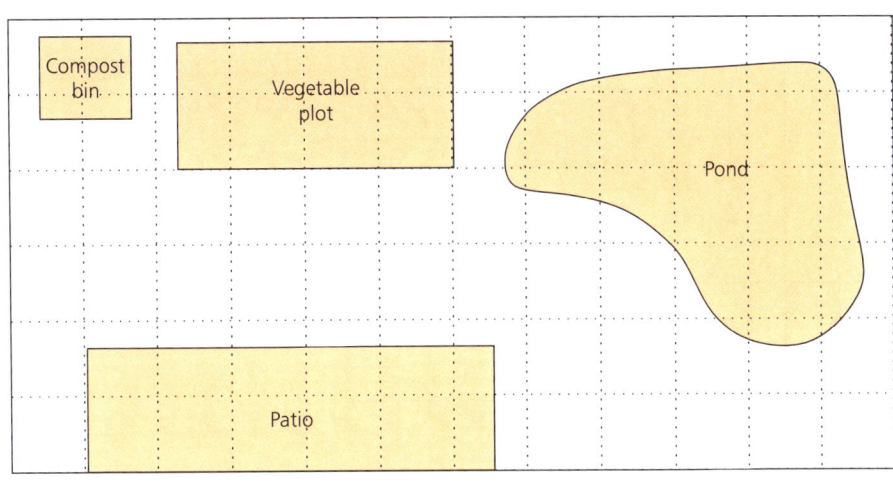

House

Mr Smith is putting a fence around the **perimeter** of his garden.

**a** From the plan find out how much fence he should buy. _____

Fencing costs £3 per metre.

**b** Write down the cost of the fence. _____

Mr Smith wants to put a safety net over the pond.

Scale: 1 cm : 5 metres

**c** Find the approximate surface area of the pond. _____

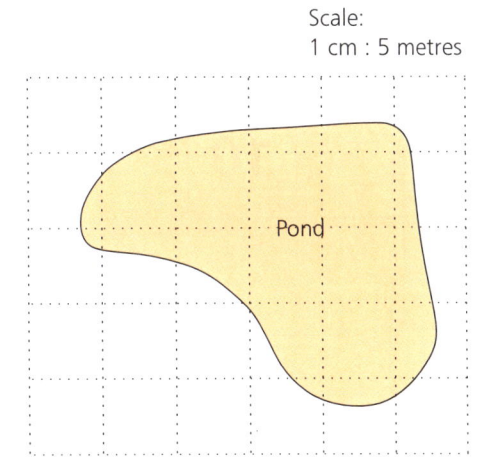

These blocks will be used to make a wall.

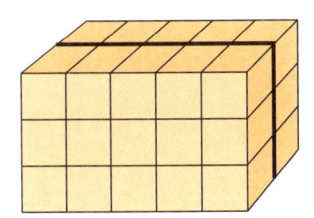

**d** How many blocks are there in the pile? _____

TOTAL (4)

# Paper 1 test

## 4 Sliding Ts

These patterns are made from T shapes.

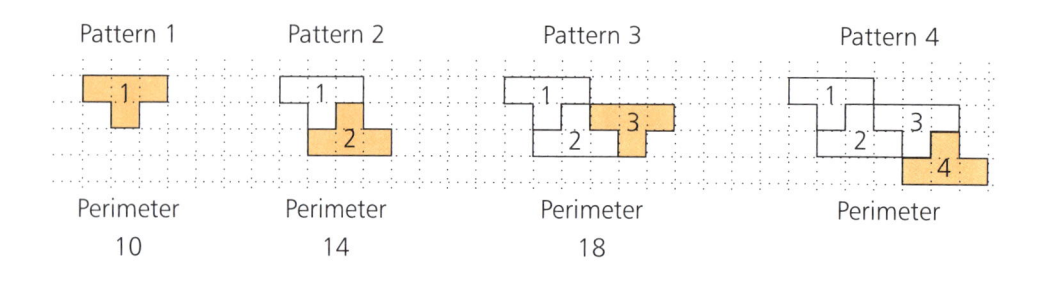

Pattern 1   Pattern 2   Pattern 3   Pattern 4

Perimeter   Perimeter   Perimeter   Perimeter
10          14          18          _____

a  Find the perimeter of pattern 4.

b  Write down the rule for finding the perimeter in words.

c  What is the perimeter of pattern 10? _____

TOTAL (3)

# Paper 1 test

## 5 Shapes

There are 20 shapes in grid A.

**A**

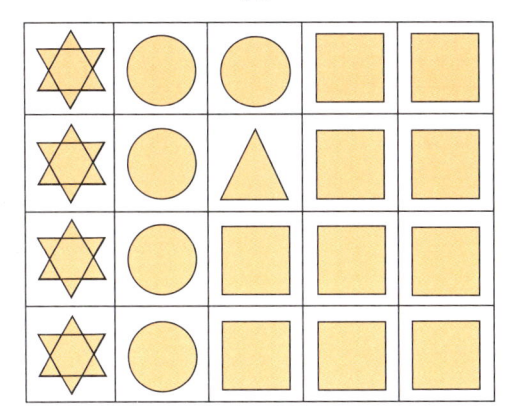

**a** What fraction of the shapes are squares? _____

**b** What fraction of the shapes are circles? _____

**c** What fraction of the shapes are stars? _____

**d** Draw triangles in $\frac{1}{5}$ of grid B.

**B**

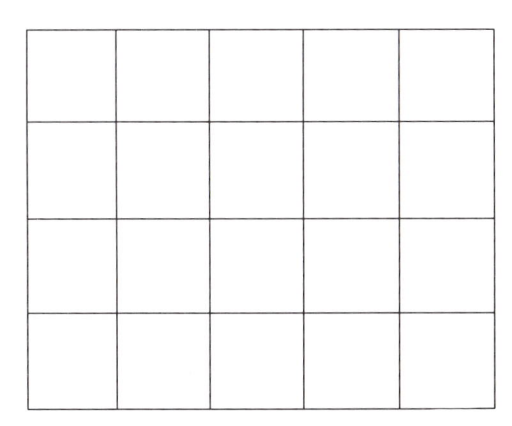

# Paper 1 test

## 6 Triangle

**a** Using compasses and a ruler, accurately draw a triangle with sides 4.5 cm, 6 cm and 7.5 cm.

**b** Measure the angles of your triangle.

Write down the size of the largest angle. _____

**c** Match these angles to their descriptions (one has been done for you).

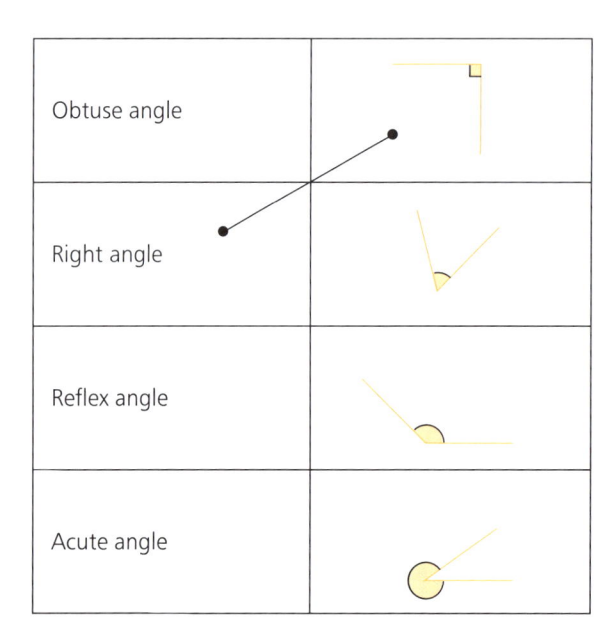

| | |
|---|---|
| Obtuse angle | |
| Right angle | |
| Reflex angle | |
| Acute angle | |

TOTAL (6)

# Paper 1 test

### 7 Random numbers

Hamish and Tom take it in turns to turn a card over from each pile.

They multiply the two numbers on the cards and add the answer to their score.

The first to 1000 wins.

Add on their scores on the score pad.

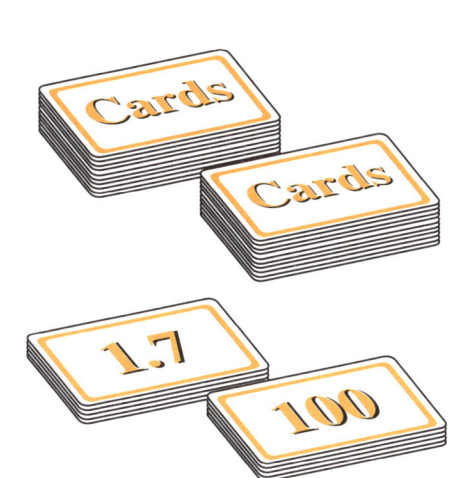

**a**

| Score Pad  First to 1000 wins |||||
|---|---|---|---|---|
| Hamish ||| Tom ||
| 13 × 10 | ~~130~~ | | 5 × 100 | ~~500~~ |
| 2.8 × 100 | ~~280~~ | | 11 × 10 | ~~110~~ |
| | 410 | | | 610 |
| 0.6 × 100 | ~~60~~ | | 1.7 × 100 | ~~170~~ |
| | 470 | | | 780 |

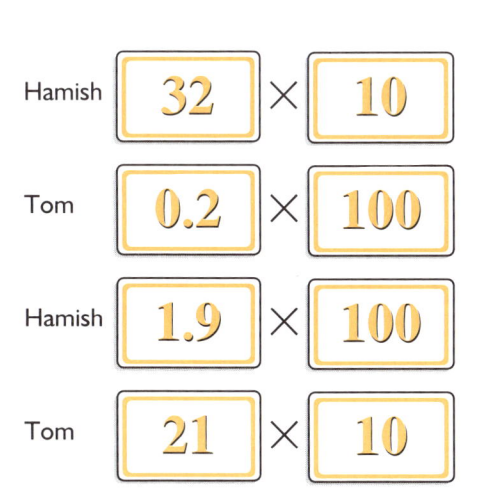

Hamish  32 × 10

Tom  0.2 × 100

Hamish  1.9 × 100

Tom  21 × 10

**b** Who won the game? _____

# Paper 1 test

## 8 Imperial

Jamila is explaining measures to her next-door neighbour, Sheila.

She puts them in a table so Sheila can see at a glance.

Complete the table.

Choose from these.

| 3 grams | ½ litre | 2 mm | 0.5 metre |
| 25 grams | 2 litres | 2.5 cm | 1 metre |
| 40 grams |  | 12.5 cm | 10 metres |

| Imperial | Metric |
| --- | --- |
| 1 lb (one pound) | 400 grams |
| 1 oz (one ounce) |  |
| 1 pint |  |
| 1" (one inch) |  |
| 1 ft (one foot) | 30 cm |
| 1 yd (one yard) |  |

These may help.

16 oz = 1 lb
12 inches = 1 foot
3 feet = 1 yard

TOTAL (2)

*Paper 1 test*

9 **Windows**

This window uses 24 panes of glass.

a How many panes of glass would 225 windows use?

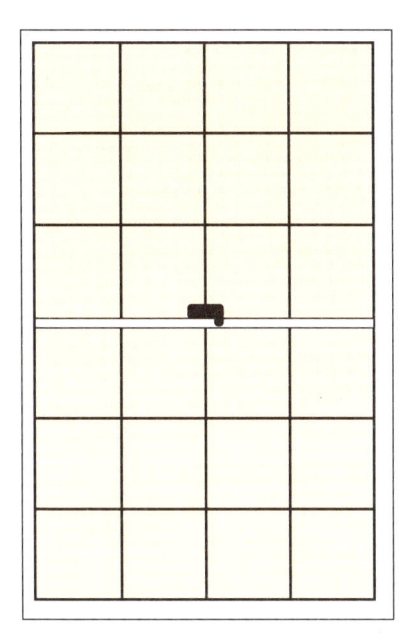

_____

This window uses 6 panes of glass.

b How many windows could be made with 2268 panes of glass?

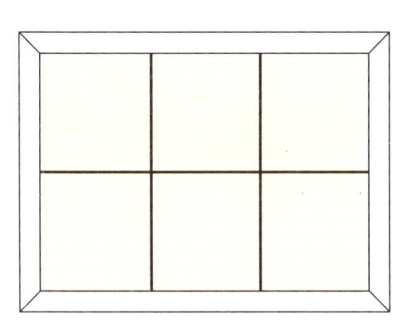

_____

c This window has reflection symmetry. Mark all the lines of symmetry on the diagram.

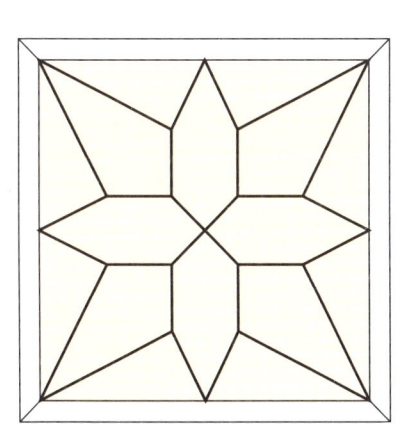

TOTAL (3)

# Paper 1 test

## 10 Probability

|————————————————————|
0                                             1

Mark each of these probabilities on the probability scale with an arrow.

**a** The probability of getting an even number when a six-sided dice is rolled.

**b** The probability of drawing a spade from a pack of cards.

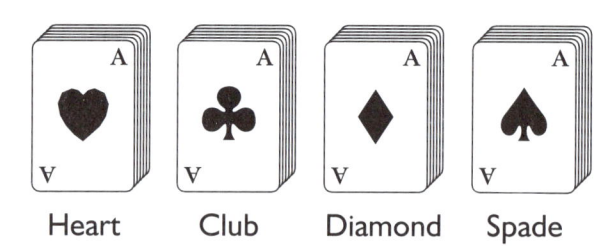

Heart   Club   Diamond   Spade

**c** The probability of getting 'blue' on the spinner.

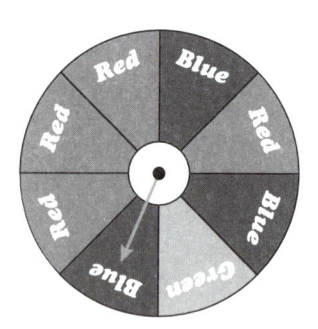

**d** The probability of choosing a white counter from a bag with these counters in it.

TOTAL (4)

# Paper 1 test

## 11 Computers

**CELL TECH** — SPECIAL OFFER! COMPUTER XB40 £999.99 + VAT @ 17.5%

**BIG BYTE** COMPUTER XB40 £1150 including VAT @ 17.5%

Cell Tech and Big Byte are selling the same computer at different prices.

**a** Find the cost of the Cell Tech computer including VAT.

**b** Which shop is offering the best deal?

**MEGA-MEDIA** COMPUTER XC80 £1800. including VAT or £81 per month for 2 years

Mega-Media have an offer of spreading the payments over 2 years.

**c** How much does the computer cost if paid for over 2 years?

**d** How much extra is this?

**e** Find the percentage increase on the original cost.

TOTAL (5)

# Paper 1 test

## 12 Pin number

Dave keeps this piece of paper in his wallet so he can work out his PIN number if he forgets it.

$$2A + 3 = 9$$

$$\frac{D}{3} + 20 = 21$$

$$2(E + 1) = 2$$

$$140 - 20V = 0$$

Solve each equation.

a  $2A + 3 = 9$

A = _____

b  $\frac{D}{3} + 20 = 21$

D = _____

c  $2(E + 1) = 2$

E = _____

d  $140 - 20V = 0$

V = _____

e  Write the answers in the table to find Dave's PIN number.

| D | A | V | E |
|---|---|---|---|
|   |   |   |   |

TOTAL (5)

# Paper 1 test

## 13 Elections

Year 9 held a mini-election. These are the results.

| Party | Votes |
|---|---|
| Conservative | 12 |
| Green | 48 |
| Labour | 24 |
| Liberal Democrats | 24 |
| Other | 12 |
| Total | 120 |

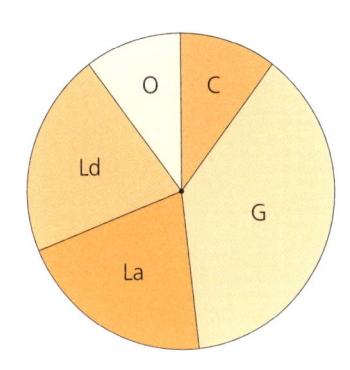

Key:
Conservative    C
Green    G
Labour    La
Liberal Democrats    Ld
Other    O

Year 8 also held a mini-election.
All the pupils voted.

| Party | Votes |
|---|---|
| Conservative | 15 |
| Green | 75 |
| Labour | 24 |
| Liberal Democrats | 24 |
| Other | 12 |

a  How many students are there in Year 8? _____

b  Draw a pie chart showing the results from the table.

c  Which year gave the largest percentage of votes to the Green Party?

TOTAL (5)

## 14 Shot put

This is a sketch of a shot put circle.

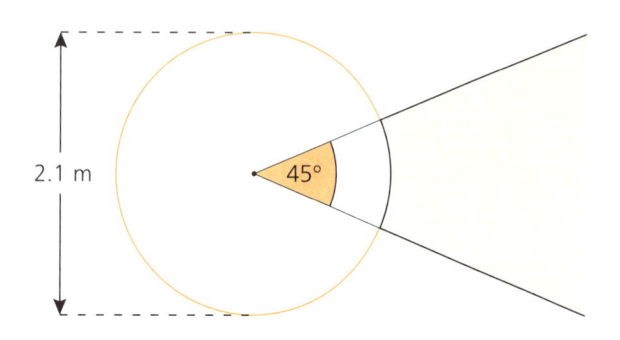

2.1 m
45°

The diameter of the circle is 2.1 metres.

a  Find the area of the circle. _____

The circle has a band of wood or metal around it.

b  Find the length of the band around the circle. _____

## 15 Parallelogram

The base of this parallelogram is 3 times as long as the height.

**a** If the height is *x* cm, write down an expression for the area of the parallelogram.

_____

**b** The area of the parallelogram is 64 cm². Use trial and improvement to find the height of the parallelogram. Give your answer to 1 decimal place.

| | Height | Area |
|---|---|---|
| 1st try | 5 | |

*x* = _____

# Paper 2

## Test Paper 2 Levels 5–7

60 Mins TIME ALLOWED

The use of calculators is permitted in this paper if you see this symbol:

This symbol: means you must not use a calculator.

### 1 Car

Jo has bought a new car.

She is going on holiday and has fitted a roof rack.

The car is 1.52 m high.

The roof rack is 35 cm high.

**a** Can Jo fit the car through the garage door?
Explain your answer.

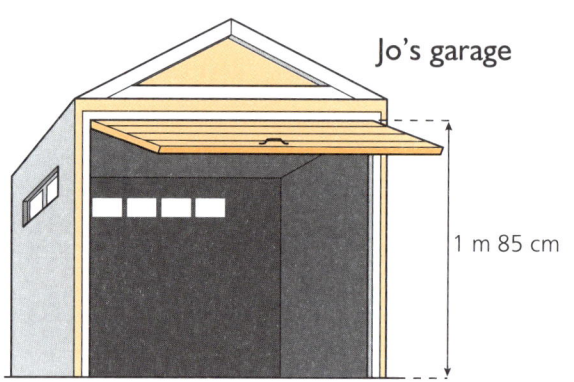

Jo's garage

1 m 85 cm

Jo fills up her car with petrol before she starts her journey.
The petrol tank holds 110 litres of petrol. At the end of the journey it is $\frac{3}{4}$ full.

**b** How many litres of petrol has she used? _____

The journey was 120 km.

**c** How many kilometres per litre does the new car do?

**d** Jo's old car did 4.25 km per litre. Which car is better value to run?
Explain your answer.

TOTAL (4)

36

# Paper 2 test

## 2 Probability

There are three methods for finding probability:

**Method 1** – carry out an experiment or collect data.

**Method 2** – use probability theory.

**Method 3** – use historical or past data.

Write down which method you would use for each of the following.

**a** The probability of winning a raffle.

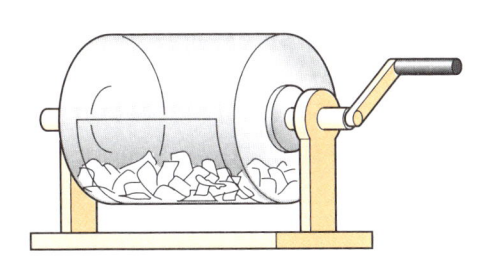

_____

**b** The probability that the number 62 bus will arrive on time.

_____

Jackie and Ali are playing spin the wheel.

They choose 2 colours each.

Jackie chooses white and red.

Ali chooses green and blue.

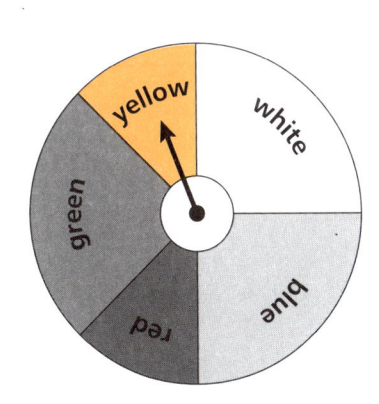

**c** What is the probability that Ali wins? _____

**d** What is the probability that neither wins? _____

TOTAL (4)

37

# Paper 2 test

### 3 News

**BOYWATCH CONCERT SELL-OUT**
25,000 FANS TURN OUT TO SEE BOYWATCH. ¾ OF FANS ARE UNDER 15.

**SHARES DOWN BY 20%**
Big Spender shares fell from £1.80 to

a How many Boywatch fans were under 15? _____

b Find the new value of Big Spender shares. _____

St Benedict's School produces a weekly school newspaper.

These are the sales for one half term.

| Week | 1 | 2 | 3 | 4 | 5 | 6 |
|---|---|---|---|---|---|---|
| Sales | 210 | 195 | 300 | 150 | 180 | 165 |

c How many papers were sold this half term? _____

d The paper sells for 20p a copy. How much money is taken altogether?
_____

e What fraction of the total papers sold were sold in week 3?
_____

TOTAL (5)

# Paper 2 test

## 4 Matchsticks

Square patterns are made from matchsticks.

1 square    2 squares    3 squares    4 squares

**a** Draw the 4 squares pattern.

**b** How many matchsticks would be needed for 10 squares? _____

**c** Complete the rule that connects the number of squares with the number of matchsticks.

Matchsticks = _____

**d** Use your rule to find out how many matchsticks are needed for 28 squares.

_____

**e** How many squares can be made from 61 matchsticks? _____

TOTAL (5)

39

# Paper 2 test

### 5 Outcomes

Helen is tossing a coin and rolling a six-sided fair dice.

**a** Complete the table to show all the possible outcomes.

|  |  | Dice | | | | | |
|---|---|---|---|---|---|---|---|
|  |  | 1 | 2 | 3 | 4 | 5 | 6 |
| **Coin** | Head | H, 1 |  |  |  |  |  |
|  | Tail |  |  | T, 3 |  |  |  |

**b** What is the probability that Helen gets a tail and an odd number?

_____

# Paper 2 test

## 6 Sports Day

In the heats of the 400 metres on Sports Day in 1998, the following times were recorded, to the nearest second.

**a** Put these results into this frequency table.

137  170  123  106  128  129
141  147  152  139  197   96
 88  156  216  161  144  163
119  178  156  146  188  153
126  149  115  154  142  172

| Time, s (seconds) | Tally | Frequency |
|---|---|---|
| $80 < s \leq 100$ | | |
| $100 < s \leq 120$ | | |
| $120 < s \leq 140$ | | |
| $140 < s \leq 160$ | | |
| $160 < s \leq 180$ | | |
| $180 < s \leq 200$ | | |
| $200 < s \leq 220$ | | |
| | Total | |

**b** How many pupils took part in the heats? _____

**c** Draw a frequency diagram on the grid below.

This is the frequency diagram from the previous year's heats for the 400 m.

**1997 400 m heat times**

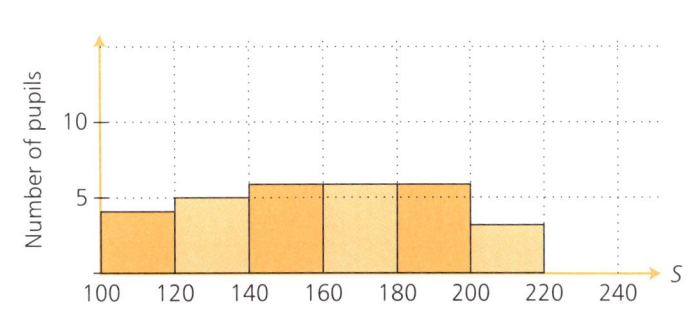

**d** Write down two differences between the results in 1997 and 1998.

TOTAL (6)

# Paper 2 test

**7 House**

Left → Right ←  4 BEDROOM 'CLEVEDON'

This is the top or plan view of the 'Clevedon'.

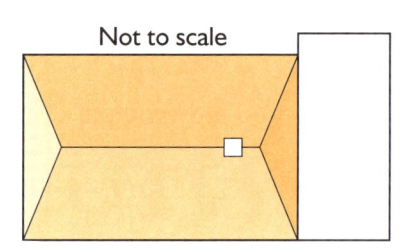

Not to scale

**a** Sketch the front view of the Clevedon.

**b** Sketch the left side view of the Clevedon.

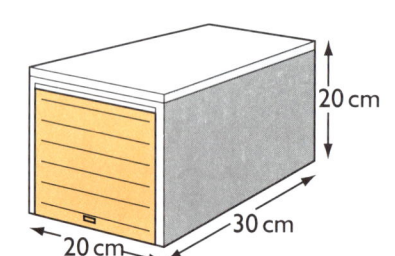

This is a model of the Clevedon garage.

20 cm
20 cm  30 cm

**c** Find the volume of the model in cubic centimetres. _____ cm³

**d** Find the volume of the model in cubic metres. _____ m³

TOTAL (4)

# Paper 2 test

## 8 Theme park

Three coach parties of people visited a theme park.

The theme park owners were studying a new ride and collected this information.

$\frac{4}{9}$ of coach A rode on BATMAN.

$\frac{5}{8}$ of coach B rode on BATMAN.

$\frac{6}{10}$ of coach C rode on BATMAN.

**a** Complete this table. Change the fractions to decimals and percentages.

| Coach | A | B | C |
|---|---|---|---|
| Fraction | $\frac{4}{9}$ | $\frac{5}{8}$ | $\frac{6}{10}$ |
| Decimal | | | |
| Percentage | | | |

**b** Which coach had the largest percentage of people who rode the BATMAN ride?

_____

**c** On another coach, 35 passengers out of 50 rode on the BATMAN ride. Write 35 out of 50 as a percentage.

_____

TOTAL (5)

43

# Paper 2 test

## 9 Machines

The vertices of a triangle ABC have co-ordinates A(2, −1), B(4, −1) and C(4, 1).

**a** Plot the points A, B and C on the graph below and join them to make a triangle.

This machine multiplies the y co-ordinate by 4.

A (2, −1) → multiply y co-ordinate by 4 → A' ( __ , __ )
B (4, −1) → → B' ( __ , __ )
C (4, 1) → → C' ( __ , __ )

**b** Find the co-ordinates of A', B' and C'. Draw the new triangle on the same graph.

**c** Describe the change made by the machine. _____

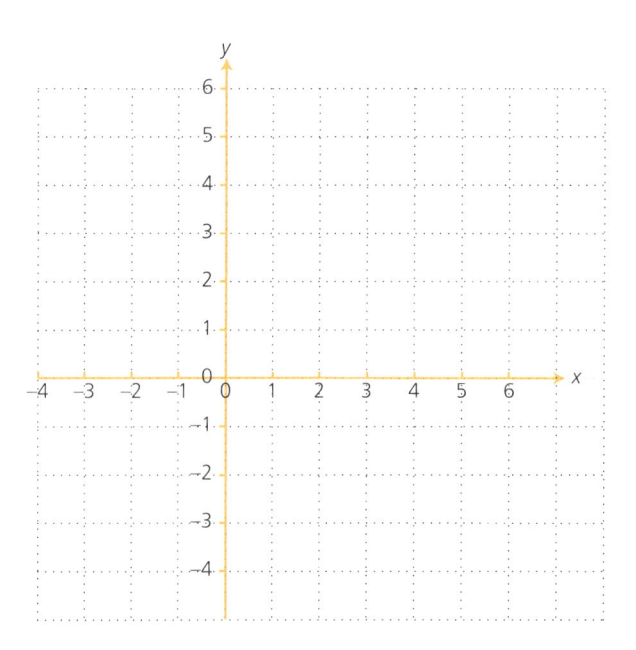

TOTAL (4)

44

*Paper 2 test*

**10 Substitution**

$a = 2 \quad b = 3 \quad c = 4$

**a** Find $\dfrac{a + c}{b}$ _____

**b** Find $ab\sqrt{c}$ _____

$x = 0.1 \quad y = 5 \quad z = 2$

**c** Find $\dfrac{yz}{x}$ _____

**d** Find $x(y+z)$ _____

TOTAL (4)

45

# Paper 2 test

## 11 Parcels

Maureen is sending a parcel to her friend in India.

She weighs the parcel.

It weighs 192 grams to the nearest gram.

a What are the minimum and maximum possible weights of the parcel to one decimal place?

Maximum possible weight _____

Minimum possible weight _____

Maureen is sending 20 identical parcels to her friends.

b **Estimate** the total weight of the 20 parcels.
Give your answer in kilograms.

# Paper 2 test

**12 Tent**

This diagram represents the front of a two-man tent.

*Not drawn to scale*

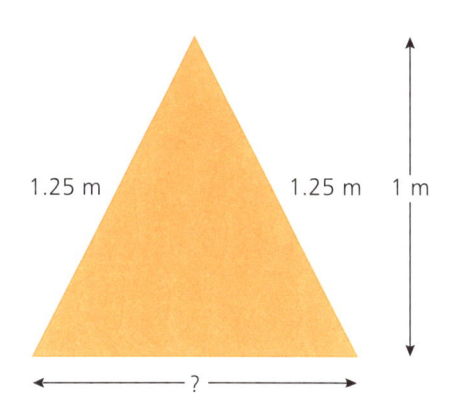

1.25 m  1.25 m  1 m

?

**a** Find the width of the tent. _____

Mr Dayley buys 150 tents for £4200.

**b** How much does one tent cost? _____

He adds on 20% profit to the price he paid when he sells the tents.

**c** How much total profit does Mr Dayley make? _____

TOTAL (4)

# Paper 2 test

## 13 Circles

Circle patterns are made from black and white counters.

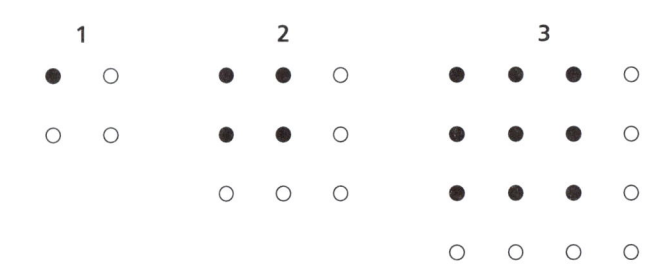

```
   1              2                    3                        4
 ● ○          ● ● ○              ● ● ● ○
 ○ ○          ● ● ○              ● ● ● ○
              ○ ○ ○              ● ● ● ○
                                 ○ ○ ○ ○
```

**a** Draw the 4th pattern.

**b** Complete the table showing the numbers of counters.

| Pattern | 1 | 2 | 3 | 4 | 5 | 6 | n |
|---|---|---|---|---|---|---|---|
| Black counters | 1 | 4 | 9 | | | | |
| White counters | 3 | 5 | 7 | | | | |
| Total counters | 4 | 9 | 16 | | | | |

**c** What is the rule for the number of black counters in the $n$th pattern?

_____

**d** What is the rule for the number of white counters in the $n$th pattern?

_____

# Paper 2 test

**14 Graph**

This table shows the values of x and y which fit the equation

$$y = x^2$$

for values between $x = -3$ and $x = 3$.

| x | −3 | −2 | −1 | 0 | 1 | 2 | 3 |
|---|---|---|---|---|---|---|---|
| y |   | 4 |   |   |   |   |   |

**a** Complete the table.

**b** Draw the graph of $y = x^2$

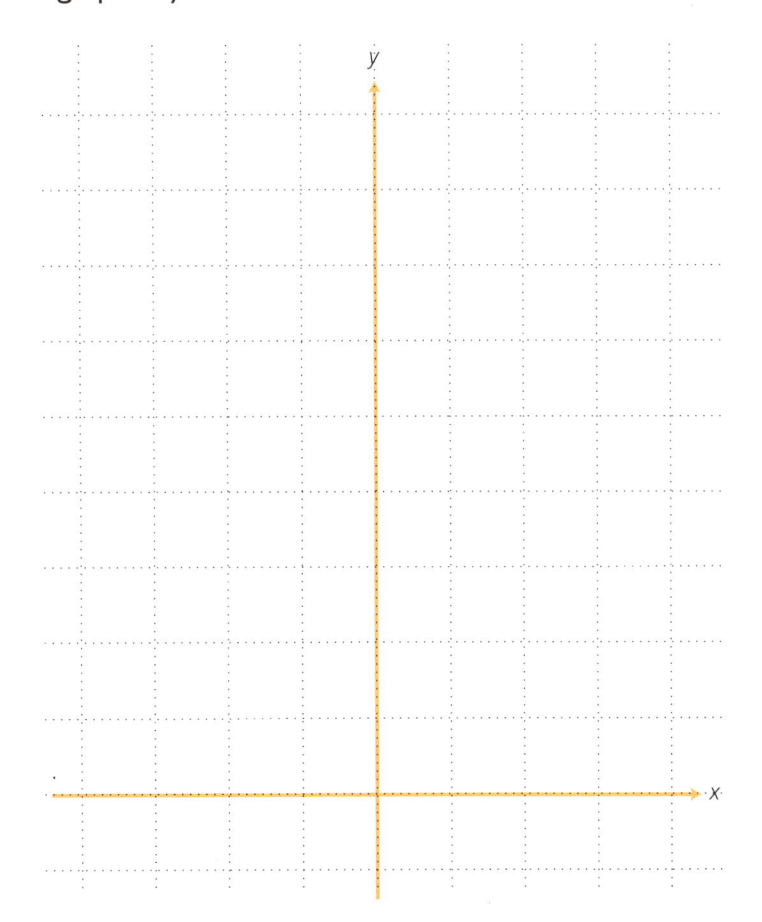

**c** Bob calculates that $y = -2.25$ when $x = -1.5$. Explain why he is wrong.

_____

_____

_____

TOTAL (4)

49

# Practice questions at Level 8

**20 Mins TIME ALLOWED**

The use of calculators is permitted in this paper if you see this symbol:

This symbol: means you must not use a calculator.

## 1 Office

Les and Mandy work in an office.

Les travels to work by train. The probability that he is late for work is $\frac{1}{4}$.

Mandy travels to work by bus. The probability that she is late for work is $\frac{1}{5}$.

**a** Find the probability that **either** Les **or** Mandy is late for work.

**b** What is the probability that they are **both** on time?

## 2 Log flume

This is a side view of part of the log flume ride at a Theme Park.

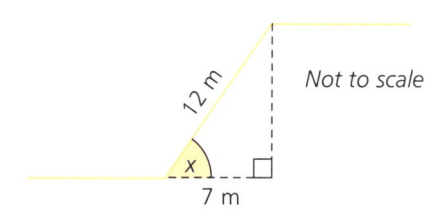

12 m
7 m
*Not to scale*
$x$

Find the angle marked $x$.

TOTAL (4)

50

# Practice questions at Level 8

## 3 Wedding

A wedding party was attended by 80 guests.
The distance travelled by each guest was recorded in a frequency table.

| Distance, d (km) | Number of guests, f | Cumulative frequency |
|---|---|---|
| $0 < d \leq 40$ | 38 | |
| $40 < d \leq 80$ | 20 | |
| $80 < d \leq 120$ | 11 | |
| $120 < d \leq 160$ | 7 | |
| $160 < d \leq 200$ | 0 | |
| $200 < d \leq 240$ | 4 | |

**a** Complete the cumulative frequency table.

**b** Draw a cumulative frequency curve below.

**c** Find the median distance travelled. _____

**d** Find the interquartile range. _____

TOTAL (5)

## Practice questions at Level 8

### 4 Million

**a** Is $(5.3 \times 10^2) \times (2 \times 10^4)$ greater or less than one million?

Give reasons for your answer. _____

_____

_____

**b** Work out the answer to

$$\frac{4.8 \times 10^2 + 3.7 \times 10^3}{2 \times 10^{-2} - 6.9 \times 10^4}$$

Give your answer in standard form to 2 significant figures.

_____

### 5 Investment

Josie invests £5000 in an investment account. She gets 6% interest at the end of each year.

**a** How much will Josie have in her account at the end of 5 years?

_____

**b** What is the percentage increase on her investment after 5 years?

_____

**c** How many years will it take for the value of the investment to reach £15 000?

_____

TOTAL (7)

52

*Practice questions at Level 8*

## 6 Plant pots

This drawing represents a plant pot holder.

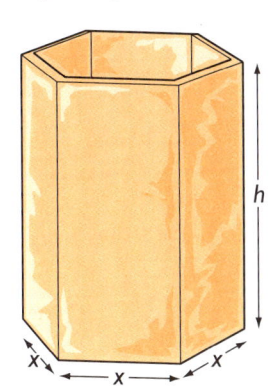

$\frac{3}{2}\sqrt{3}\, x^2 h^2$

$\frac{3}{2}\sqrt{3}\, x^2 h$

$\frac{3}{2}\sqrt{3}\, x^2 + 6xh$

$\frac{3}{2}\sqrt{3}\, x$

$\frac{3}{2}\sqrt{3}\, x^2 h^2 + 6x$

$\frac{3}{2}\sqrt{3}\, x + 6xh$

**a** Which of the expressions could be for the **surface area** of the plant pot holder?

_____

**b** Which of the expressions could be for the **volume** of the plant pot holder?

_____

This plant pot holder is a cylinder.

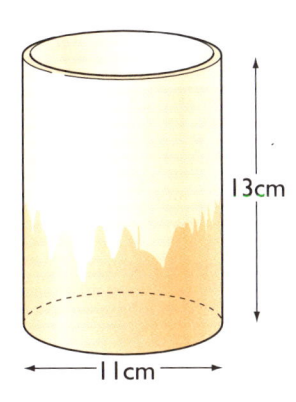

13 cm

11 cm

**c** Calculate the volume of the container.

_____

**d** Write the volume in litres. _____ litres

**e** Find the surface area of the container.

_____

_____

TOTAL (6)

53

# Answers

## Mental Test 1

1. 34
2. 1000 m
3. $32\frac{1}{2}$ (or 32.5)
4. 48
5. 5014
6. 180 min
7. 220
8. **A** grey
   **B** black
9. £3.45
10. **A** 39
    **B** 69
11. 6900
12. **A** between 30 and 35%
    **B** 50%
13. **A** $p = 9$
    **B** $p = 12$
14. £35
15. £5.02
16. 6 min
17. 8 cm
18. −8
19. **A** 12 cm²
    **B** 8 cm²
20. **A** 34
    **B** 38
21. **A** 40°
    **B** 70°
22. £27.50
23. 1.62 m or 1 m 62 cm
24. 10.25 p.m. or 10:25 or 22:25 or 25 past 10
25. **A** Shape B (a square)
    **B** Shape C (a square)
26. **A** 0.9  0.1  (0.4)
    **B** (0.4)  0.2  0.8
27. **A** 384
    **B** 384
28. 37
29. **A** 18 cm
    **B** 21 cm
30. **A** 40 cm²
    **B** 32 cm²

# Answers

## Mental Test 2

1. 480
2. 0.2
3. $\frac{6}{10} = \frac{3}{5}$ or 0.6 or 60%
4. 350 cm
5. 8.4
6. 60
7. **A** 40
   **B** 80
8. **A** $2x + 2y$ or $2(x + y)$
   **B** $2x - 2y$ or $2(x - y)$
9. There is an infinite number of fractions that are equivalent to $\frac{3}{4}$:
   $\frac{6}{8}, \frac{9}{12}, \frac{12}{16}, \frac{15}{20}, \frac{18}{24}$, etc.
10. **A** 8 cm²
    **B** 7.5 cm² (or $7\frac{1}{2}$ cm²)
11. **A** $q = 20$
    **B** $q = 25$
12. 0.15
13. 13
14. **A** $y = 9$ or $-9$
    **B** $y = 8$ or $-8$
15. **A** $4x - 2x^2$
    **B** $3x - 4x^2$
16. **A** Approximately $200 \times 40 = 8000$
    **B** Approximately $200 \times 40 = 8000$
17. $30 \times 60 = 1800$
18. **A** 15
    **B** 27
19. 854
20. **A** 17, 21, 13, (18), 22
    **B** 12, 17, 18, 10, (15)
21. 229.6
22. 136
23. 62°
24. $x = 4$ and $y = 7$ or $x = 7$ and $y = 4$
25. 100 mph
26. **A** (first shape circled)
    **B** (first shape circled)
27. **A** $\frac{1}{2}$ or $\frac{3}{6}$
    **B** $\frac{1}{3}$ or $\frac{2}{6}$
28. 700
29. **A** 30 cm²
    **B** 37.5 cm² or $37\frac{1}{2}$ cm²
30. 600

# Answers
## Practice questions at Level 3

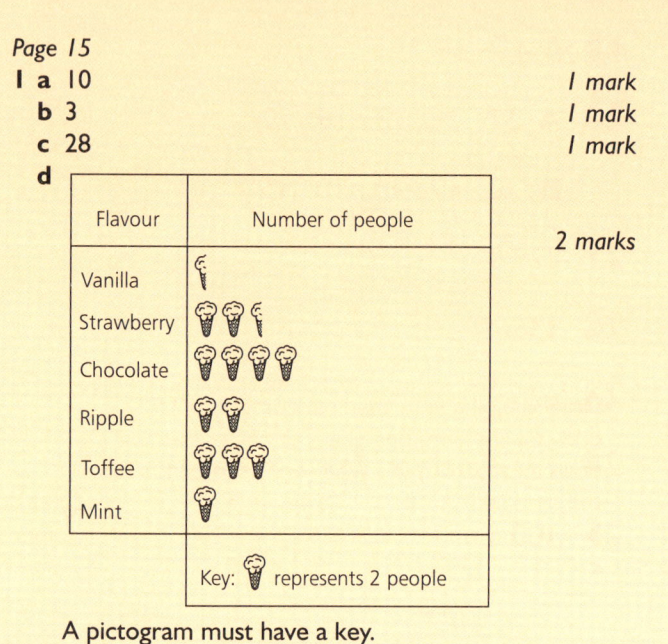

Page 15
1 a 10     1 mark
  b 3     1 mark
  c 28     1 mark
  d     2 marks

| Flavour | Number of people |
|---|---|
| Vanilla | 🍦 |
| Strawberry | 🍦🍦🍦 |
| Chocolate | 🍦🍦🍦 |
| Ripple | 🍦🍦 |
| Toffee | 🍦🍦🍦 |
| Mint | 🍦 |

Key: 🍦 represents 2 people

A pictogram must have a key.

Page 17
2 a  $2\frac{1}{2}$ hours or 2.5 hours or 2 hours 30 minutes    1 mark
  b  37 minutes    1 mark
  c  £61 + £5 + £5 + £5 = £76    1 mark

Page 18
3

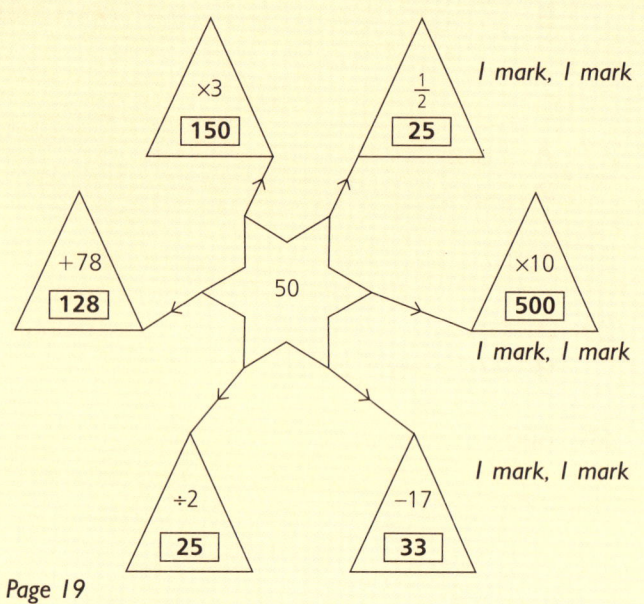

×3 → 150    1 mark, 1 mark
½ → 25
+78 → 128
50
×10 → 500    1 mark, 1 mark
÷2 → 25    1 mark, 1 mark
−17 → 33

Page 19
4 a     1 mark

| −7 | −6 | −5 | −4 | −3 | −2 | −1 | 0 | 1 | 2 | 3 | 4 | 5 | 6 | 7 |
|---|---|---|---|---|---|---|---|---|---|---|---|---|---|---|
|  |  |  |  |  | Ⓒ |  |  |  |  |  | Ⓣ |  |  |  |

  b −4     1 mark
  c Trevor     1 mark

Page 20
5 a     2 marks

  b 18     1 mark

56

# Answers

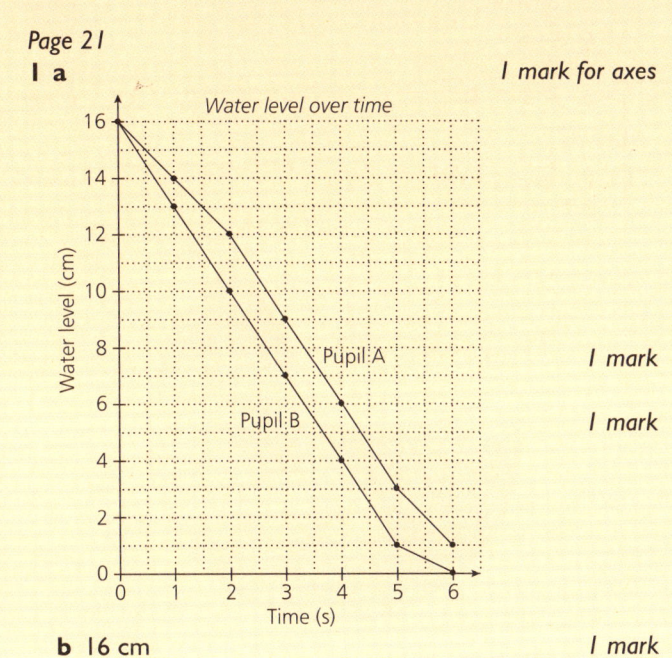

## Paper 1

**Page 21**

**1 a**  *1 mark for axes*

Water level over time graph showing Pupil A and Pupil B

  *1 mark* (Pupil A)
  *1 mark* (Pupil B)

**b** 16 cm  *1 mark*

**c** Pupil B's results are in a straight line, except at the very end, which means the water was emptying at a constant rate, while Pupil A's results aren't OR Pupil B's water level dropped more quickly than Pupil A's.  *1 mark*

**Page 22**

**2 a** Factors of 36 (numbers which divide into 36 without a remainder).  *1 mark*
**b** Multiples of 5  *1 mark*
**c** Square numbers  *1 mark*

**Page 23**

**3 a** 12 cm + 6 cm + 12 cm + 6 cm = 36 cm
  36 × 5 = 180 metres  *1 mark*
**b** 3 × 180 = £540  *1 mark*
**c** Approximately 11 squares.
  Each square is 25 m²
  Area = 11 × 25 = 275 m²  *1 mark*
**d** 30 blocks  *1 mark*

**Page 24**

**4 a** Perimeter = 22  *1 mark*
**b** Add four each time OR four times the pattern number add 6  *1 mark*
**c** 4 × 10 + 6 = 46  *1 mark*

**Page 25**

**5 a** $\frac{10}{20} = \frac{1}{2}$  *1 mark*
**b** $\frac{5}{20} = \frac{1}{4}$  *1 mark*
**c** $\frac{4}{20} = \frac{1}{5}$  *1 mark*
**d**   *1 mark*

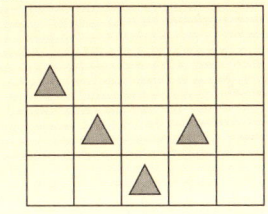

Triangles drawn in any 4 cells in the grid. This is one example.

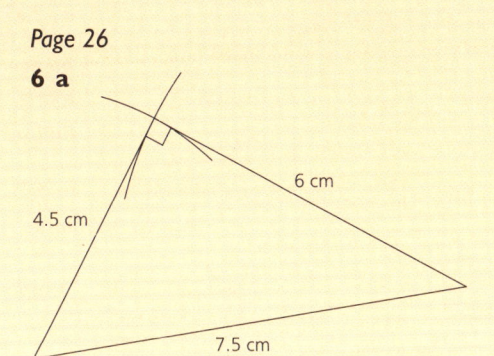

**Page 26**

**6 a**

Triangle with sides 4.5 cm, 6 cm, 7.5 cm with right angle marked

Draw one line first, then set compasses to draw an arc from one end. Set compasses to draw an arc from the other end then complete the triangle. Can start with any side.  *2 marks*
**b** 90°  *1 mark*
**c**   *3 marks*

| Obtuse angle | |
| Right angle | |
| Reflex angle | |
| Acute angle | |

**Page 27**

**7 a**

| Score Pad  First to 1000 wins |||||
|---|---|---|---|
| Hamish || Tom ||
| 13 × 10 | ~~130~~ | 5 × 100 | ~~500~~ |
| 2.8 × 100 | 280 | 11 × 10 | ~~110~~ |
|  | 410 |  | 610 |
| 0.6 × 100 | ~~60~~ | 1.7 × 100 | ~~170~~ |
|  | 470 |  | 780 |
| 32 × 10 | ~~320~~ | 0.2 × 100 | ~~20~~ |
|  | 790 |  | 800 |
| 1.9 × 100 | ~~190~~ | 21 × 10 | ~~210~~ |
|  | 980 |  | 1010 |

*1 mark, 1 mark* (for 32 × 10 row)
*1 mark, 1 mark* (for 1.9 × 100 row)

**b** Tom  *1 mark*

57

# Answers Paper 1

Page 28
8

| Imperial | Metric |
|---|---|
| 1 lb (one pound) | 400 grams |
| 1 oz (one ounce) | **25 grams** |
| 1 pint | **½ litre** |
| 1" (one inch) | **2.5 cm** |
| 1 ft (one foot) | 30 cm |
| 1 yd (one yard) | **1 metre** |

½ mark (for 25 grams)
½ mark (for ½ litre)
½ mark (for 2.5 cm)
½ mark (for 1 metre)

Page 29

9 a
```
    225
  ×  24
   ----
    900
   4500
   ----
   5400
```
5400 panes  1 mark

b
```
      378
  6 ) 2268
```
378 windows  1 mark

c  1 mark

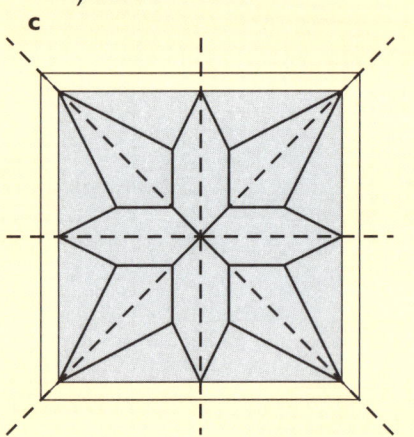

Page 30

10  (b) (c) (a) (d)  4 marks

$\frac{1}{4}$  $\frac{3}{8}$  $\frac{1}{2}$  $\frac{6}{7}$

0 ———————————— 1

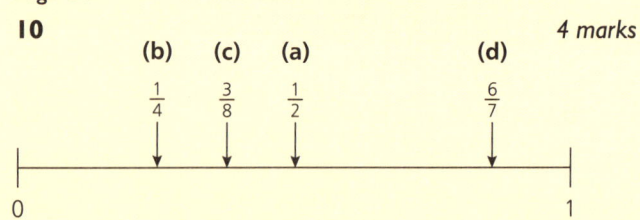

Page 31

11 a £999.99 × 1.175 = £1174.99
   to the nearest 1p  1 mark
   b Big Byte gives the best deal.  1 mark
   c £81 × 24 months = £1944  1 mark
   d £1944 − £1800 = £144  1 mark
   e $\frac{144}{1800} \times 100 = 8\%$  1 mark

Page 32

12 a A = 3  1 mark
   b D = 3  1 mark
   c E = 0  1 mark
   d V = 7  1 mark
   e 3 3 7 0  1 mark

Page 33

13 a 150 students  1 mark
   b  2 marks

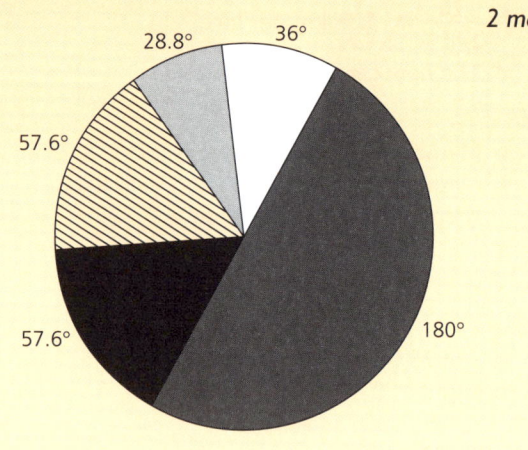

Key:
☐ = Conservative
■ = Green
▨ = Other
▧ = Lib Dem
■ = Labour

Angles: 36°, 28.8°, 57.6°, 57.6°, 180°

Every pie chart should have a key but you can choose your own. You can draw the sections in any order.

   c Year 8  1 mark

Page 34

14 a A = $\pi r^2$
   (using π button on calculator) = 3.46 m²  1 mark
   (2 dp)
   b C = $\pi d$
   (using π button on calculator) = 6.60 m  1 mark
   (2 dp)

Page 35

15 a Area = $x \times 3x = 3x^2$  1 mark
   Remember the base is 3 times the height.
   b  2 marks

| | Height (x) | Area (3x²) | |
|---|---|---|---|
| 1st try | 5 | 75 | ✗ |
| 2nd try | 4 | 48 | ✗ |
| 3rd try | 4.5 | 60.75 | ✗ |
| 4th try | 4.6 | 63.48 | ✗ |
| 5th try | 4.7 | 66.27 | |

x = 4.6 to 1 decimal place.

# Answers

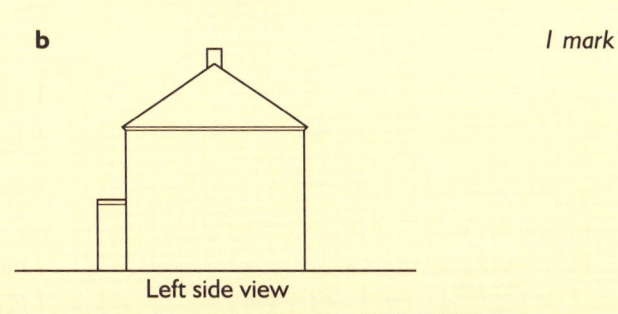

## Paper 2

*Page 36*

**1 a** 1.52 m + 35 cm = 1.87 m
Garage = 1.85 m
No it won't fit, by 2 cm. — *1 mark*
**b** $\frac{1}{4}$ of 110 = 27.5 litres — *1 mark*
**c** $\frac{120}{27.5}$ = 4.36 km per litre — *1 mark*
**d** The new car uses less petrol. — *1 mark*

*Page 37*

**2 a** Method 2, probability theory. — *1 mark*
**b** Method 1 unless there is data available, then you could use method 3. — *1 mark*
**c** $\frac{1}{4} + \frac{1}{4} = \frac{1}{2}$ — *1 mark*
**d** $\frac{1}{8}$ — *1 mark*

*Page 38*

**3 a** $\frac{3}{4}$ of 25 000 = 18 750 people — *1 mark*
**b** £1.80 × 0.8 = £1.44 per share
or find 20% and subtract
£1.80 × 0.2 = £0.36
£1.80 − £0.36 = £1.44 — *1 mark*
**c** 210 + 195 + 300 + 150 + 180 + 165 = 1200 — *1 mark*
**d** 1200 × 20p = 24 000p = £240 — *1 mark*
**e** $\frac{300}{1200} = \frac{1}{4}$ — *1 mark*

*Page 39*

**4 a** — *1 mark* 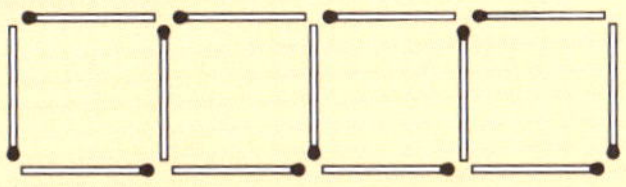
**b** 31 matchsticks — *1 mark*
**c** Matchsticks = 3 × squares + 1
or = 3s + 1 — *1 mark*
**d** m = 3 × 28 + 1
= 85 — *1 mark*
**e** 61 = 3s + 1
60 = 3s
20 = s      20 squares — *1 mark*

*Page 40*

**5 a** — *1 mark*

|  | Dice | | | | | |
|---|---|---|---|---|---|---|
|  | 1 | 2 | 3 | 4 | 5 | 6 |
| Coin Head | H, 1 | H, 2 | H, 3 | H, 4 | H, 5 | H, 6 |
| Coin Tail | **T, 1** | T, 2 | **T, 3** | T, 4 | **T, 5** | T, 6 |

**b** $p$ (T, odd) = $\frac{3}{12} = \frac{1}{4}$ — *1 mark*

*Page 41*

**6 a** — *2 marks*

| Time, s (seconds) | Tally | Frequency |
|---|---|---|
| 80 < s ≤ 100 | || | 2 |
| 100 < s ≤ 120 | ||| | 3 |
| 120 < s ≤ 140 | ℍ| | | 6 |
| 140 < s ≤ 160 | ℍ| ℍ| | | 11 |
| 160 < s ≤ 180 | ℍ| | 5 |
| 180 < s ≤ 200 | || | 2 |
| 200 < s ≤ 220 | | | 1 |
| Total |  | 30 |

**b** 30 — *1 mark*
**c** — *1 mark*

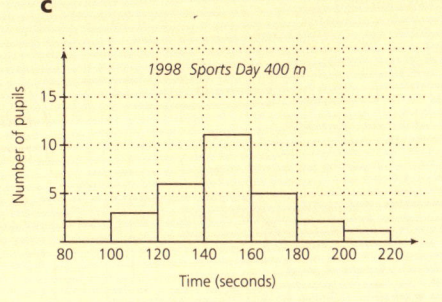

**d** In 1998 the range increased; AND the times in 1997 were more evenly spread. — *2 marks*

*Page 42*

**7 a** — *1 mark*
**b** — *1 mark*
**c** 20 cm × 20 cm × 30 cm = 12 000 cm³ — *1 mark*
**d** 0.2 m × 0.2 m × 0.3 m = 0.012 m³ — *1 mark*

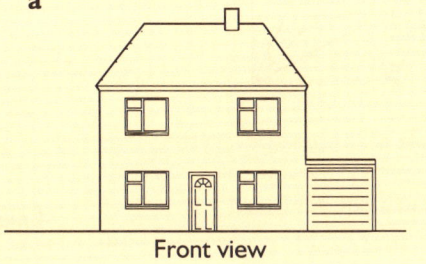

# Answers Paper 2

*Page 43*

**8 a**

| Coach | A | B | C |
|---|---|---|---|
| Fraction | $\frac{4}{9}$ | $\frac{5}{8}$ | $\frac{6}{10}$ |
| Decimal | 0.4̇ | 0.625 | 0.6 |
| Percentage | 44.4̇% | 62.5% | 60% |

*3 marks*

**b** Coach B — *1 mark*

**c** $\frac{35}{50} = 70\%$ — *1 mark*

*Page 44*

**9 a** (Triangle ABC) — *1 mark*
(Triangle A'B'C') — *1 mark*

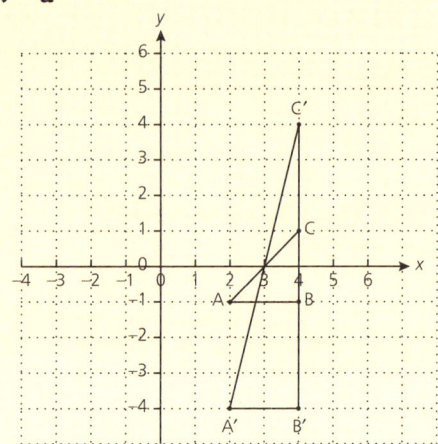

**b** — *1 mark*

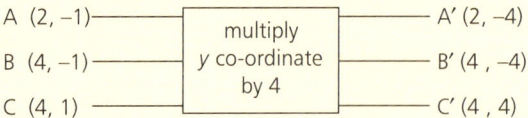

A (2, −1) ⟶ multiply y co-ordinate by 4 ⟶ A' (2, −4)
B (4, −1) ⟶ ⟶ B' (4, −4)
C (4, 1) ⟶ ⟶ C' (4, 4)

**c** The triangle is stretched along the y-axis and is four times the size vertically. You may write this in a different way! — *1 mark*

*Page 45*

**10 a** $\frac{2+4}{3} = 2$ — *1 mark*

**b** $2 \times 3 \times \sqrt{4} = 12$ or $-12$ — *1 mark*

**c** $\frac{5 \times 2}{0.1} = \frac{10}{0.1} = 100$ — *1 mark*

**d** $0.1(5 + 2) = 0.7$ — *1 mark*

*Page 46*

**11 a** Minimum 191.5 grams — *1 mark*
Maximum 192.5 grams — *1 mark*
This is often shown like this:
$191.5 \leq w < 192.5$ grams

**b** 20 × 200 g = 4000 grams
= 4 kg — *1 mark*

*Page 47*

**12 a** Use Pythagoras' theorem.

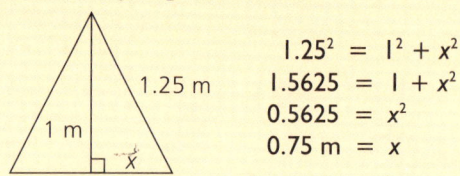

$1.25^2 = 1^2 + x^2$
$1.5625 = 1 + x^2$
$0.5625 = x^2$
$0.75$ m $= x$

The tent is 2 × 0.75 m = 1.5 m wide — *2 marks*

**b** £4200 ÷ 150 = £28 — *1 mark*

**c** £4200 × 0.2 = £840 — *1 mark*

*Page 48*

**13 a** — *1 mark*

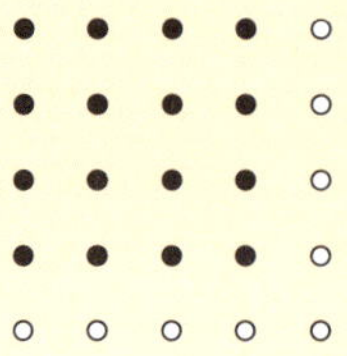

**b** — *2 marks*

| Pattern | 1 | 2 | 3 | 4 | 5 | 6 | n |
|---|---|---|---|---|---|---|---|
| Black counters | 1 | 4 | 9 | **16** | **25** | 36 | $n^2$ |
| White counters | 3 | 5 | 7 | **9** | 11 | 13 | $2n + 1$ |
| Total counters | 4 | 9 | 16 | **25** | **36** | 49 | $n^2 + 2n + 1$ |

**c** B = number of black counters. $B = n^2$
You may have written 'square numbers' or multiplied by itself, but you need to write the rule using algebraic notation. — *1 mark*

**d** W = number of white counters
$W = 2n + 1$ — *1 mark*

*Page 49*

**14 a** — *1 mark*

| x | −3 | −2 | −1 | 0 | 1 | 2 | 3 |
|---|---|---|---|---|---|---|---|
| y | 9 | 4 | 1 | 0 | 1 | 4 | 9 |

**b** — *2 marks*

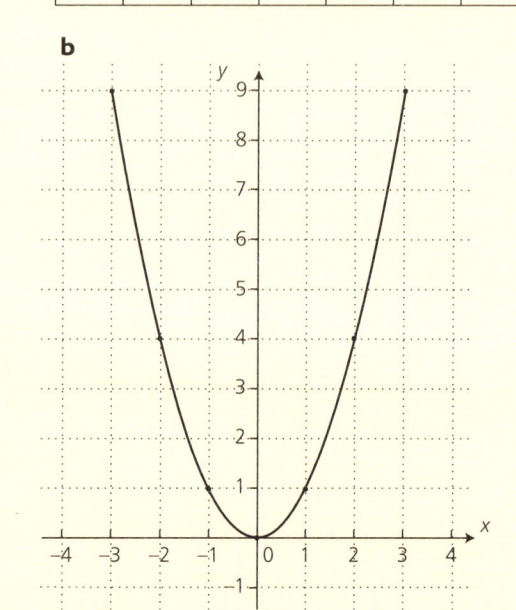

**c** When $x = -1.5$ the value of y lies between 1 and 4
OR $y = x^2$ and all squares are positive. — *1 mark*

# Answers

## Practice questions at Level 8

*Page 50*

**1 a** $\left(\frac{1}{4} \times \frac{4}{5}\right) + \left(\frac{3}{4} \times \frac{1}{5}\right) = \frac{7}{20}$
or 0.35 or 35%  *1 mark*

**b** $\frac{3}{4} \times \frac{4}{5} = \frac{12}{20} = \frac{3}{5}$
or 0.6 or 60%  *1 mark*

**2** $\cos x = \frac{7}{12} = 0.583$  $x = 54.3°$ (1 dp)  *2 marks*

*Page 51*

**3 a**  *1 mark*

| Distance, d (km) | Number of guests, f | Cumulative frequency |
|---|---|---|
| 0 < d ≤ 40 | 38 | 38 |
| 40 < d ≤ 80 | 20 | 58 |
| 80 < d ≤ 120 | 11 | 69 |
| 120 < d ≤ 160 | 7 | 76 |
| 160 < d ≤ 200 | 0 | 76 |
| 200 < d ≤ 240 | 4 | 80 |

**b**  *2 marks*

Distance travelled by wedding guests (cumulative frequency graph)

**c** Median distance is about 43 miles.  *1 mark*
**d** Interquartile range is about 85 − 18 = 67 km.
Your results may be slightly different but still correct.  *1 mark*

*Page 52*

**4 a** $(5.3 \times 10^2) \times (2 \times 10^4) = 1.06 \times 10^7$
1 million = $1 \times 10^6$ so $1.06 \times 10^7$ is greater than a million.  *2 marks*
**b** $-6.1 \times 10^{-2}$  *1 mark*

**5 a** After 1 year  $5000 \times 1.06$
After 2 years  $5000 \times (1.06)^2$
After 3 years  $5000 \times (1.06)^3$
After 4 years  $5000 \times (1.06)^4$
After 5 years  $5000 \times (1.06)^5 = £6691.13$  *1 mark*

**b** $\frac{1691.13}{5000} \times 100 = 33.82\%$  *1 mark*

**c** $5000 \times (1.06)^n = 15\,000$
Try values of n until you just go over 15 000
e.g. $5000 \times (1.06)^{18} = 14\,271.70$
$5000 \times (1.06)^{19} = 15\,128.00$
19 years  *2 marks*

*Page 53*

**6 a** $\frac{3}{2}\sqrt{3}x^2 + 6xh$  *1 mark*

**b** $\frac{3}{2}\sqrt{3}x^2h$  *1 mark*

**c** V  $= \pi r^2 h$
$= \pi \times 5.5^2 \times 13$
$= 1235.43$ cm³ (using π button on calculator)
or 1234.81 cm³ (using π = 3.14)  *1 mark*

**d** 1.235 litres  *1 mark*
(Remember 1000 cm³ = 1 litre)

**e** Base  $= \pi r^2$
$= \pi \times 5.5^2$
$= 95.03$ cm² (using π button on calculator)
or 94.99 cm² (using π = 3.14)
Sides  = circumference × height
$= \pi \times d \times h$
$= \pi \times 11 \times 13$
$= 449.25$ cm² (using π button on calculator)
or 449.02 (using π = 3.14)
Surface area = 95.03 + 449.25 cm²
$= 544.28$ cm²
or 544.01 (using π = 3.14)  *2 marks*

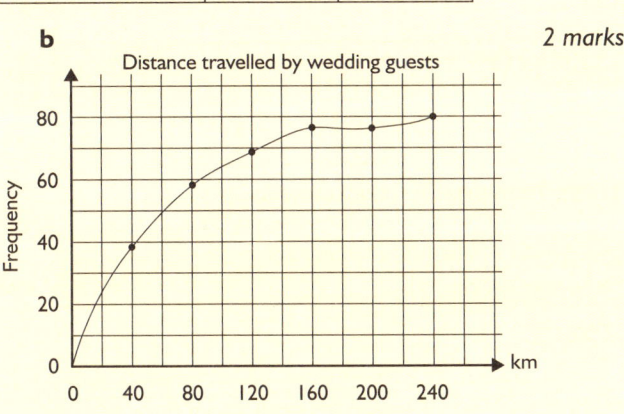

61

# National Curriculum levels

## Converting the score into National Curriculum levels

1 Look at the questions which your child has got right:

| | |
|---|---|
| **Practice questions at Level 3** | Level 3 |
| **Paper 1** questions 1–5 | Level 4 |
| questions 6–10 | Level 5 |
| questions 11–15 | Level 6 |
| **Paper 2** questions 1–5 | Level 5 |
| questions 6–9 | Level 6 |
| questions 10–14 | Level 7 |
| **Practice questions at Level 8** | Level 8 |

2 Numerical scores can be used to give an approximate National Curriculum level.

| Practice questions at Level 3: maximum marks available 20 | |
|---|---|
| Working at Level 3 with some areas still to be addressed | 11–15 |
| Secure at Level 3 | 16–20 |

| Paper 1: maximum marks available 59 | |
|---|---|
| Some work at Level 4 but with many areas to be addressed | less than 15 |
| Working at Level 4 and towards Level 5 | 16–29 |
| Working at Level 5 and towards Level 6 | 30–39 |
| Working at Level 6 | 40–50 |
| Secure at Level 6 | 51+ |

## National Curriculum levels

| Paper 2: maximum marks available 59 ||
|---|---|
| Some work at Level 5 but with many areas to be addressed | less than 15 |
| Working at Level 5 and towards Level 6 | 16–29 |
| Working at Level 6 and towards Level 7 | 30–39 |
| Working at Level 7 | 40–50 |
| Secure at Level 7 | 51+ |

| Practice questions at Level 8: maximum marks available 22 ||
|---|---|
| Working at Level 8 but with some areas to be addressed | 11–15 |
| Secure at Level 8 | 16–22 |

| Mental Test 1 |
|---|
| The paper is targeted at Levels 3–5. |

| Mental Test 2 |
|---|
| The paper is targeted at Levels 5–6 although it contains a few questions at Levels 4 and 7. |
| A satisfactory mark on either mental test is 16 or over. |

# Notes